Florence Nightingale
God's Servant at the Battlefield

Florence went against the wishes of her wealthy parents and defied social custom when she took up a career that no respectable woman of that day would even consider. She became a nurse.

History knows her now as "The Lady with the Lamp." Night after night she walked among the cots of wounded soldiers, carrying her kerosene lamp to light the darkness and wearing her cape to keep out the cold. She was always ready to bandage the wounds of a bleeding soldier, give a drink of water to a thirsty patient, or write a letter home for a private on his deathbed.

Up until Florence's time, the hospitals in England were a disgrace. Could she better conditions? She would have to overcome the resistance of high officials, the apathy of the public, and even the ignorance of doctors.

Throughout her life, Florence remembered the entry in her diary when she was still a girl: "God spoke to me and called me to His service."

About the Author

David R. Collins is an award-winning author who has written numerous books for young people, including Sower Series *Abraham Lincoln*, *George Washington Carver*, and *Francis Scott Key*.

For many years Mr. Collins has taught English to high school boys and girls. He enjoys helping them get acquainted with Charles Dickens and William Shakespeare, as well as more recent authors.

About the Artist

Edward Ostendorf, known as Ned O., says, "I started drawing before I could write my name. I had a big brother who was an artist, and I thought that was the neatest thing on earth. I grew up knowing I would be an artist and attended every art class after school and on Saturday that I could find." Since then he has gone on to illustrate everything from newspapers to books.

Florence Nightingale

God's Servant at the Battlefield

by

David R. Collins

Illustrated by **Edward Ostendorf**

MOTT MEDIA

All Scriptures are from the King James Version of the Bible.

Louise H. Rock, Editor
A. G. Smith, Cover Artist

LIBRARY OF CONGRESS CATALOGING IN PUBLICATION DATA

Collins, David R.
    Florence Nightingale: God's Servant at the Battlefield

    (Sowers Series)
    Bibliography: p. 147
    Includes index.

    SUMMARY: A biography of the well-to-do woman who defied social convention in order to establish nursing as a respectable career for women and bring about reforms in hospital conditions and nursing care.
        1. Nightingale, Florence 1820-1910—Juvenile literature. 2. Nurses—England—Biography—Juvenile literature. [1. Nightingale, Florence, 1820-1910. 2. Nurses.] I. Ostendorf, Ned, ill. II. Title. III. Series.

RT37.N5C65   1985   610.73'092'4 [B] [92]   84-60316
ISBN 0-88062-126-5   Paperbound

CONTENTS

INTRODUCTION

Prejudice.

Ignorance.

Waste.

These were obstacles faced by Florence Nightingale. She found them early in childhood and she battled them all her life. By the time she finished, Florence Nightingale had lifted the nursing profession to a level of admiration and respect.

Surprisingly enough, young Florence Nightingale might have enjoyed a life of pleasure and comfort. Her parents had wealth and position. There was no need for Florence to experience a moment's distress.

But something planted itself deep within Florence. In her diary, she noted, ''God spoke to me and called me to His service.'' It was a call she answered with a deep love shown by sacrifice and devotion for others. To countless soldiers, she became known as God's servant on the battlefield.

Today, in every country of the world, people who are sick and injured may receive proper care and attention. They owe much to Florence Nightingale, who heard God's call to service and answered it.

Call to Service

"Wasn't that a delightful party?" Mrs. Nightingale exclaimed as she slipped off her jeweled cloak. Her husband handed the cloak to a servant, then led the way into the family parlor. The two Nightingale sisters, Parthenope and Florence, trailed behind.

"I've never had a more wonderful time," gushed Parthe, the older of the two girls. She twirled around the room in the arms of a make-believe partner. Her golden brown curls bobbed up and down on her shoulders.

"And what about you, Florence? Did you enjoy yourself, too?" Mrs. Nightingale seated herself by her younger daughter and warmly took her hand.

"Yes, it was a very nice party, Mother."

"I should say she thought it was nice. Didn't you see her dancing, Mother?" Parthe couldn't resist the temptation to tease. "There were gentlemen lined up all the way across London Bridge."

Mr. Nightingale had started a crackling fire in the fireplace and slowly lighted a long Danish pipe. For several minutes he stood watching his family busily chattering. Then he sat down in a low stuffed chair.

"I am the one who can say it was a wonderful party," Mr. Nightingale announced proudly. "Of course, who else can claim to escort the three prettiest ladies in England?"

"Thank you, kind sir." Parthe curtsied to her father and then planted a grateful kiss on his forehead.

Mrs. Nightingale rose from the sofa and crossed to the blazing fire.

"Did any of you happen to hear some news about Her Majesty?" she asked. "One of the ladies mentioned that there has been a frequent caller at the palace lately . . . a Prince Albert I believe she said."

"Yes, that's what I heard too!" Parthe exclaimed. "He's her cousin from Germany. Some were saying that it wouldn't be long before they announced plans for a marriage. Wouldn't that be gorgeous? Little Queen Victoria of England and a prince from Germany!"

"Well, I suggest you two little ladies run along to bed." Mr. Nightingale tapped the ashes from his pipe into the fireplace. "Tomorrow it will be our turn to entertain and you will want to be fresh for the occasion."

"Yes, let's go up, Flo. I haven't had a chance to show you the new bracelet I picked out today." Parthe tugged at her sister's hand, but Florence did not budge.

"Mother, Father." Florence paused. "May I please be excused from the party tomorrow? I am sure Parthe could entertain the guests and I would probably not even be missed."

"Florence Nightingale! How can you even think of such a thing? This is your last chance to entertain before we leave Embley Park!" her mother said.

"But why must we always have a party before we go away for the summer?" Florence asked. "Would it be so strange if we just left without telling the entire city we are going?"

Mrs. Nightingale gasped. Go away without having a party? Why, the idea was ridiculous! Such action would violate the strict rules of London society in 1839.

"We *have* to give a party whenever we go away for any length of time. Florence, why can't you accept the responsibility like your friends and Parthe?" Mrs. Nightingale scolded.

"Because I see no purpose in giving a party unless one finds it enjoyable. Why must we feel we *have* to entertain, regardless of whether we want to or not?"

"It's too late to argue tonight, Florence. I'm certain you'll feel differently about this in the morning. I suggest you get a good night's rest."

Florence knew no further discussion was possible. Sadly she joined Parthe and went off to bed.

But in the morning, Florence did not feel differently. As she dressed, she could hear the servants busily working downstairs. Flinging herself across the bed, she rolled over and stared up at the pink ceiling. "How strange this world is!" she said. "Parties . . . dances . . . piano lessons . . . They're all so senseless and boring."

Surely there was more to life than this!

Florence stood up and crossed the room to her dresser. She picked up the small black book marked *Diary* and glumly read some of the entries.

July 16, 1835 . . . Spent the day arranging flowers.
September 17, 1836 . . . Took a carriage ride with
    Mother.
October 14, 1836 . . . Tried to paint a scene with
    watercolors—horrible results!

January 10, 1837 . . . Parthe and I hosted a tea party.
   Dull.

Entry after entry read the same—just a long chain
of boring days. Then, came an entry recorded on
February 7, 1837.

God spoke to me and called me to His service.

For several moments Florence stared at the words.
Her skin seemed to tingle with excitement as she
recalled the night she had made the entry. She had
been sleeping when she thought she heard a strange
voice. Immediately she had taken her diary and
recorded the words.

Florence slammed the diary on the dresser. It was
over two years ago that she had made that important
entry in her diary! Now, at the age of eighteen, she
still had done nothing about it. Her thoughts were
interrupted by Parthe's voice at the doorway.

"Flo, mother wants you to come downstairs and
help with the silverware. It must all be counted and
polished. I've got to pick some fresh flowers."

"I'll be down in a few minutes. I want to write a
letter first."

"Well, hurry as fast as you can. All the silverware
must be counted and polished before five o'clock."

"It will be, don't worry."

Florence searched through the dresser drawer to
find a quill. Locating one, she seated herself at her
writing desk and began her letter.

Dearest Aunt Mai,

   We are making our plans now to leave for Lea
Hurst. Do you think it might be possible for me to
come and visit you soon? Please do not think me rude
for requesting an invitation, but you have always said
that I was welcome any time I wanted to come. I wish
to talk with you about several things.

Mother and Father are fine, as is Parthe.

Your loving niece,
Florence

As Florence carefully addressed the envelope, she wished she could have written everything she wanted to tell her aunt. Aunt Mai always listened and tried to understand. Now Florence needed desperately to talk to someone.

Carrying the letter, Florence hurried downstairs where she found a hectic state of confusion. She could hear her mother's voice in the parlor. When she reached the parlor entrance, Florence stopped in surprise. Mrs. Nightingale was perched on a ladder trying to hang garlands of flowers from a chandelier. The flowers were wrapped around her neck in a huge necklace fashion and her eyes were barely visible at the top.

"May I help you, Mother?" Florence offered.

"Yes, yes." Mrs. Nightingale's voice was muffled through the flowers. "Hurry into the kitchen, Florence. It's getting late. You must begin counting the silverware. It must be polished, too. I hate to have you do it instead of the servants, but they are busy."

"Yes, Mother."

"And see if you can find Parthe. Send her in here. It was her idea to have flowers hanging on the chandeliers, but she certainly isn't much help at carrying her ideas through. I just don't understand how this can be done."

"Has anyone taken the letters, Mother?"

"No, Clarence will take them shortly. Just lay it on the table. And please see about the silver, Florence."

Florence met Parthe in the kitchen. Clarence, the Nightingale butler, was also there, so she handed him her letter.

"Mother's looking for you, Parthe. She's having some problems with the flowers over the chandeliers."

"I know she's having problems. I've been hiding from her all morning. If she thinks I'm going to climb that ladder, I'm afraid she's mistaken."

"But didn't you suggest it, Parthe? If you don't want it done. . ."

"Oh, I think it would look nice, but I don't want to—"

". . . do it myself." Florence ended her sister's sentence. Florence walked to the kitchen table and opened the large case containing silverware. Parthe trailed behind her.

"But Flo, you don't understand. I just don't like to climb ladders. I get nervous when—"

"Parthe, don't explain to me. Every time we have a party, you find an excuse for getting out of the work."

"Well, at least I don't bury myself in a Latin book or sit around working mathematical problems all the time."

"Let's not argue, Parthe. Mother asked to see you and I relayed her message. Now I have to get this silverware counted and polished."

"Oh, I wish we weren't going to have a party!" said Parthe, as she slipped through the kitchen door.

"And I hope it will be the last one for some time," Florence whispered under her breath.

Royal Wedding

"Florence . . . Flor-ence. Please come downstairs. A letter has come for you."

Hearing her mother's call, Florence closed her book and jumped from her bed. She hurried down the steps, taking two at a time.

"Now, my dear young daughter, you will return to the top of the stairs and descend them gracefully."

"But what about my letter, Mother? May I see it, please?"

"Not until you do as I have asked. Your father may feel that all knowledge comes from books, but I feel some other things are also important, especially manners."

"All right, Mother." Florence walked up the staircase, then returned, being very careful to hold her head aloft.

"Fine, Florence. You have such a beauty about you. I only wish you weren't so set in your ideas." Mrs. Nightingale handed her daughter the letter, then went to her sewing in the parlor.

Florence recognized the writing immediately.

"It's from Aunt Mai!" she exclaimed. Rushing up the stairs, she ripped it open, and read it eagerly.

My darling Florence,

So nice to receive your letter. I am feeling fine and so happy to hear the same of you and your family.

Please ask your mother if you might come to London soon. There are so many exciting activities taking place now. You have probably heard about little Victoria. She has announced her marriage plans with Prince Albert. Everyone had expected it, but now that it is going to happen, the excitement is everywhere. I'm certain your mother would want you to come.

Let me know of your plans.

Love,
Aunt Mai

With a squeal of delight Florence twirled around the room, and finally collapsed on her bed.

"Are you all right, Miss Florence?"

Florence looked up to see Clarence standing at the doorway.

"All right? Clarence, I feel wonderful. Did you know Queen Victoria is going to be married? And did you know Aunt Mai wants me to go to London with her? And I'll also get—"

"Slow down, Miss Florence. You'll wear yourself out just talking about it." Clarence smiled and turned to go.

"Wait, Clarence." Florence raced to her closet and pulled a light blue velvet dress from it. Holding it against herself, she posed in front of the mirror.

"I've never worn this dress before. Do you think it will look all right for the wedding?"

"Why, in that dress, no one will even notice the queen." Clarence grinned and left the doorway.

Florence stared at herself for several minutes. She was tall and erect. She piled the red-gold hair on top of her head, fastening it with a silver hair clasp. Her soft gray eyes sparkled with joy.

"And how are you today, my lovely young daughter?"

Florence turned to find her father watching her. She ran and kissed him on the cheek.

"Oh, Father," she exlaimed, "I just received a letter from Aunt Mai. She's invited me to London with her. Queen Victoria and Prince Albert are going to be married. Can you imagine what a wonderful sight that will be in Westminster? I do hope you and Mother will let me go."

"It's something every English girl should see. I think Parthe may go with your cousins. But how strange for *you* to receive a letter from Aunt Mai. Usually she writes to *us* first." Mr. Nightingale's eyes had a teasing twinkle in them.

"We-ll . . . I did write a note to Aunt Mai. Father, I want to see her. I know you and Mother try very hard to understand me, but I—"

"That's all right, Florence. I knew you had been thinking about something for quite a while. I had a feeling you wanted to visit Aunt Mai. You know, I used to go to her for advice quite a bit when I was a boy, too. She's a good listener."

"Oh, I'm so glad you understand, Father. I hope Mother will."

"I have a feeling she'll be quite pleased to have you in the midst of London society at this time. She may be expecting you to bring home a French prince yourself! Perhaps, at least a British admiral."

"Father, shame on you." Florence couldn't help but laugh at her father's teasing. He bowed low before her, winked, then left the room.

"There's so much to do! I'd best start getting things in order."

Two weeks later, a horse-drawn carriage sat stacked with clothes and trunks in front of the Nightingale summer home. As Florence waved goodbye, she prayed silently that she might be saying goodbye to the life she had been leading. Through her visit to Aunt Mai's house, she hoped to find a new way of living.

London was buzzing with activity. Parties were being given everywhere. The visitor from Lea Hurst found herself quickly thrown into the busy routine of a wealthy and pretty young socialite. Gloomily, Florence realized she had found no escape. She had merely fallen into the same pattern of living in new surroundings.

Back at Lea Hurst, Mrs. Nightingale was overjoyed to hear of her daughter's success in London society. She anxiously waited to hear more of Florence's activities, hoping to learn that Florence had found a suitor worthy of the family name.

"I would like to please Mother, but I just cannot say that I have any real interest in marriage," Florence confided in Aunt Mai. "There are so many other things I'd like to do. I've found some books on mathematics that simply amaze me. Do you think I might begin taking some lessons in mathematics?"

"I'm afraid your mother won't be too pleased with the idea," said Aunt Mai with a sigh. "Perhaps I can help you with the mathematics, but you'll have to continue attending the parties. Otherwise, your mother will order you home."

Mrs. Nightingale did *not* like the idea of Florence taking mathematics.

"Why should *you* study mathematics?" she wrote in a letter. "There is no reason for a person in your position to study such a thing. How can you keep up with your important duties while spending time on such nonsense!''

Florence tried patiently to make her mother understand, but it was useless. Soon Mrs. Nightingale sent word for her daughter to return home. Florence hated to leave Aunt Mai, for they both were enjoying their new undertaking.

A flourish of parties welcomed Florence home. Every night she attended a different social function given by some Nightingale friend. How boring these parties were, until—

"May I have the pleasure of this dance, Miss Nightingale?"

Florence looked up at the handsome young gentleman who was extending his hand. He smiled, revealing two deep dimples on his cheeks.

"Why, certainly." Florence took his hand and they whirled around the floor in a delightful waltz.

"I've been trying to meet you for some time, Miss Nightingale. My name is Richard Monckton Milnes. I hadn't planned to come to this dinner party, but when I heard you were going to be present, I changed my mind."

Florence was surprised at the man's boldness. Yet it was flattering to know he was attending because of her. "I believe I have heard of you also, Mr. Milnes. I think we were in London at the same time."

"But, sadly, never in the same place at the same time, I regret to say." He smiled at her. "It seemed that every party I went to, you had been there the night before."

"It was a busy season, wasn't it?"

Florence couldn't help but like this young man. For some time she had heard stories of the dashing Richard Milnes. Supposedly he was the most eligible bachelor in all England.

"I understand you are a poet, Mr. Milnes."

"Let us just say I do a little writing. I'm afraid most of my scribblings are carted out in trash disposers."

"You're far too modest. And don't you also do something with politics?"

"Nothing worth mentioning. I've taken an interest in trying to do something with young people who are tossed into the same institutions with vicious criminals. I'm afraid it's rather an endless struggle."

"But a worthwhile one, I'm sure. Father reads my sister and me the London Times every morning."

"Not the entire newspaper, I hope?"

"Every word, I believe. Your name is often mentioned in connection with your crusade. I admire your efforts. And I agree with them too."

"Well, that is kind to hear, Miss Nightingale. I

have strong feelings we shall become good friends.''

As the months went by, Richard Milnes soon became a frequent caller to the Nightingale home. Florence's father and mother encouraged their daughter to devote her interests to him.

Yet Florence had mixed feelings. ''Richard is a wonderful person. But somehow I have little desire to be his wife. He does so many good things, things I would like to do also. I wonder if I hold only admiration for him. If so, I don't think that is enough for marriage.''

Mrs. Nightingale was impatient with Florence. Monckton Milnes was heir to a huge English estate, was a popular rising politician, and was very much in love with Florence. How could any young girl of twenty-two refuse a proposal from such a fine gentleman?

''Why would you pass up such an opportunity?'' Mrs. Nightingale asked. ''People in England are starving everywhere. It is difficult to find employment. You have the courtship of a man who will never be bothered by such things. Yet you will not accept him.''

''But Mother, that is the point. People are starving. People are without work. I'd like to help them as Richard does. I just haven't found the way I can.''

Finally, in the fall of 1842, Florence found her way.

While visiting the German ambassador, a family friend, Florence asked about his country. She wanted to know how one person, even a woman, might help ease the suffering of poor people.

''Well, I might tell you about one person who has accomplished a great deal,'' the ambassador answered. ''A Lutheran pastor named Fliedner built a small hut over in Kaiserwerth. He started taking in orphan children. Soon, he had several women helping him. It wasn't long before he and the women had constructed several large buildings to care for the boys and girls. Now they are handling hundreds of orphans and people who are poor and sick."

"And these women—they are nurses?" Florence asked.

"Yes, they do a fine job. I know you people in England have a lowly opinion of female nurses. You think women are too weak in character, too frail physically. Still, having seen the work of the Kaiserwerth nurses, I can testify that nursing could be a highly respected profession for men or for women. In my mind, one might be doing the work of the Lord in helping His people here on earth."

For a moment Florence was speechless. "Doing the work of the Lord," the ambassador had said. Could this have anything to do with the message Florence had received many months ago? She remembered the words in her diary, "God spoke to me and called me to His service." Nursing—surely this was serving! And didn't the ambassador say he thought the work of the nurses was "the work of the Lord"? Florence's body tingled with excitement.

"Do you—do you think *I* might be suited to be a nurse?" Florence asked haltingly.

The ambassador smiled. "Only you can decide that. It would be your decision—yours alone."

An Important Decision

As the months rolled by, Florence became more and more displeased with her life. Every night she went to a dinner party or dance, but this was not the only cause of her discomfort. She was saddened to see suffering people on the London streets as her elegant carriage took her to a warm and beautiful home. It just didn't seem right.

"If it bothers you to see such things, why don't you come with me on my charity calls?" suggested Mrs. Nightingale. "Maybe there is something you can do to help."

Florence accepted eagerly. This would be her chance personally to help the poor and suffering.

Mrs. Nightingale was admired by everyone for helping the servants living on her estates. As she visited each small cottage, she carried huge baskets of fruit and clothing. Florence was warmly welcomed by each family.

As they made more and more calls, Mrs. Nightingale became somewhat concerned with her daughter's interest in the poor people. Instead of merely leaving the gifts at each house, Florence wanted to stay and do other things. Often she would take a broom and begin sweeping. Sometimes, she would ask to feed the sick person herself. Such tasks were certainly below the stature of a wealthy young English lady!

"Florence, how can you force yourself to do such things?" Mrs. Nightingale inquired after an afternoon of charity calls.

"I'm not forcing myself to do them," Florence replied. "I think I would have to force myself to stop. For the first time in my life, I feel as if I am helping someone."

"But what does Richard say about your activities? Surely he does not approve."

"Richard is not in a position to approve or disapprove. I have told him that he had best find someone else who can enjoy his life. He is a great man, and I am happy to say that I know him. But I don't feel it would be fair to him for the courtship to continue."

"Oh, Florence! I only hope you won't regret your decision."

As Florence lay in bed that night, she too hoped she would not regret her decision. It was not easy to tell Richard goodbye. With him, she would always have been comfortable. But now she felt she finally knew what her life was meant to be. She chuckled to herself as she recalled the old German ambassador and his suggestion that she be a nurse. This would be her calling. It would not be easy to tell her family the news.

"Nursing" was an ugly word around England in 1844. Women who became nurses were those who could find no other type of work. Many of them drank heavily and paid little attention to their patients. Hospitals were filthy. Only the poorest people came to them, for the wealthier citizens chose to stay in their clean homes.

Florence knew that her parents would have many objections to the idea of nursing. Carefully she planned how she would offer the suggestion to them.

In the summer of 1844, the Nightingales remained at Embley Park, rather than traveling to Lea Hurst. They were planning to entertain several distinguished visitors from America.

"We just can't have them at Lea Hurst," Mrs. Nightingale explained. "It's too small there. At least we have fifteen bedrooms here at Embley. That should be enough."

Florence learned, much to her delight, that one of the guests would be Dr. Samuel Howe. She hoped to gain support for her nursing plans, and surely a doctor would support her plan.

Dr. Howe arrived with his wife, Julia, a charming woman who would later write "The Battle Hymn of the Republic." Both of them were impressed with the lovely and intelligent Florence Nightingale. Seeing her chance, Florence invited Dr. Howe to have breakfast with her.

The next morning, as Dr. Howe quietly sipped a glass of orange juice, Florence revealed her plan.

"Please do not laugh, Dr. Howe, but I want to ask you a question. Do you think it would be unsuitable for a young English woman to devote herself to works of charity in hospitals, as Catholic sisters do? Do you think it would be a dreadful thing?"

Dr. Howe stared at Florence for several seconds and set his glass on the table.

"My dear Miss Florence, it would be unusual, and in England whatever is unusual is thought to be unsuitable. But I say to you, go forward if you have a vocation for that way of life. Choose, go on with it wherever it may lead you, and God be with you.''

Florence breathed a deep sigh. She had hoped Dr. Howe might give some encouragement, but this was wonderful!

''Thank you so much, Dr. Howe. You have been very kind.''

Florence told no one of her talk with Dr. Howe. He had given her confidence, but still she had to decide how best to discuss her plans with the family. She prayed for God's help.

Within the next year, Florence was able to show her family that she really could bring comfort to sick people. Mr. Nightingale's mother was taken very ill, and Florence offered to care for her. The family agreed and were soon amazed at the old woman's recovery.

''I'd never have lived had it not been for sweet Florence,'' the elderly Mrs. Nightingale said.

Soon after, the kind and faithful Mrs. Gale, Parthe and Flo's old nurse, entered her final illness. Florence hurried to the old lady and brought much comfort before she died.

After a few days' rest, Florence learned that there was much illness in the Wellow Village, just a short distance from Embley Park. She hurriedly gathered some things in a carriage and hastened there.

It was not long before Florence learned an important thing. The sick people of Wellow Village had taught her a lesson.

''A nurse must be tender, kind, and patient with the sick,'' she told a friend. ''But a nurse must also be trained. It is not possible to help a sick person properly unless you also understand medicine and disease.''

Florence realized that the time had come for her to tell her family that she had decided to become a nurse. She knew this news would not be easy to accept.

Florence was right.

"How can you think of disgracing us this way!" Mrs. Nightingale exclaimed. "You'll ruin us!"

"Florence, you just don't care anything about us at all!" said Parthe. "If you did, you wouldn't think of doing such a thing."

Even Mr. Nightingale, whom Florence had hoped might understand, was furious with the idea.

"You're an ungrateful and disgusting wretch!" he told her. "The idea is completely ridiculous. I can't stand even to stay in the same house with a girl who would suggest such a thing." With that, Mr. Nightingale stormed out, leaving his daughter crying.

"But don't you understand?" Florence pleaded, "I want to become a nurse, a *good* nurse."

"There is no such thing as a good nurse!" Mrs. Nightingale wailed. "All of them are terrible creatures. You've seen those horrid hospitals, full of terrible smells and dirt. You've had so many advantages, Florence. How can you even think of wasting your education, your beauty, your *life* by being a nurse?"

"But it's what I want, Mother. I won't be wasting these things. I think it's what God wants me to do."

The battle raged on. For weeks, few words were spoken between Florence and her family. She hated having Parthe and her parents feel the way they did, but she knew she could not give in. "Please help them understand me, Lord," she prayed daily.

Early in the morning and late at night, Florence collected information about hospitals and nursing. She wrote everywhere for materials. Her friends in government posts supplied many pamphlets and papers. She filled notebook after notebook with information.

Mrs. Nightingale decided that if Florence had more to do she would forget about her foolish idea of becoming a nurse. So she placed Florence in charge of the linen, china, and other household equipment. With a huge house such as Embley Park, this was no easy task. Sadly Florence obeyed her mother's wishes.

One October morning, as Florence was counting saucers in the pantry, she heard Clarence in the hall. She found him picking up a pile of papers scattered on the floor.

"I'm sorry, Miss Florence. Everything seemed to flip out of my hands."

Kneeling to help the old butler, Florence smiled.

"That's all right, Clarence. I was starting to feel my eyes were turning to saucers after counting so many. Do you realize we have one hundred and ten saucers on the second shelf in the pantry?"

"No, I had no idea. You certainly know the facts about this house, Miss Florence."

"Oh, and such important facts too, Clarence," said Florence. "Some time I'll let you know how many bedsheets we have. There, I guess that's everything."

"These papers are for you, Miss Florence, and this book too. I believe they're from the German ambassador."

"Why, yes, they are. Let's take them up to my room, Clarence. We'll put them on my bed."

Later, Florence spread all the mail out on top of her bed. There were charts, pictures, sketches, and a large book entitled *The Year Book of the Institution of Deaconesses at Kaiserwerth*. She read every scrap the ambassador had sent her.

"This is grand!" she burst out. "Surely Mother and Father would let me study nursing in Kaiserwerth. This is the answer to all my plans. Oh, Lord, I knew you were listening to my prayers."

For the time being, Florence kept her hopes secret. Mrs. Nightingale was in the midst of the social party season. It would be no use to discuss the idea of Kaiserwerth now.

Florence read about Kaiserwerth whenever she found a free moment. Her desire to go there grew stronger and stronger. Yet, there never seemed to come the proper time to discuss the matter. And then there was Richard.

With romantic energy, Richard renewed his courtship. Though Florence tried to discourage him, he would not listen. The Nightingale family joined him in trying to persuade Florence to accept his offer of marriage.

By 1847, Florence was confused and sick. By Christmas, she was making plans to visit Italy with a friend, Selina Bracebridge.

"You'll enjoy the trip," Selina had promised. "It's easier to see the answers to your problems when you're

away from them awhile. Please come with us to Italy.''

Florence agreed.

Italy proved to be a wonderful vacation for Florence. The weather, the beautiful sights, the new friends—all helped the English visitor find her health.

While walking one Sunday afternoon, Selina and Florence saw a couple several yards ahead of them.

''Liz! Liz Herbert!'' Selina called.

The woman ahead turned and ran to Selina. Her husband followed. In a few minutes, Florence had met Liz and Sidney Herbert. Though Florence liked the new couple from the first meeting, she little realized how important this meeting would be to her own future.

Sidney Herbert was a tall, handsome man with a quick mind and a fine sense of humor. He was well-known in the British political scene, having been Secretary of War.

''I've heard so much about you, Mr. Herbert,'' Florence commented. ''The London Times carries so much news about your activities.''

''And often not so flattering!'' Mr. Herbert chuckled.

''On the contrary, I can't recall reading anything against you. What are your present plans?''

''Well, I—''

''Don't get him started,'' Liz Herbert interrupted. ''He will keep you here for hours with a speech.''

''I suppose she's right. Perhaps we might have dinner together.''

''When he knows he has a listener, he'll—''

This time it was Mr. Herbert who stopped his wife's joke. ''Perhaps we could travel through Italy together? How long do you plan to stay here in Rome?''

''Until Thursday,'' Selina replied.

"We plan to go to Naples next. Was that to be one of your stops?"

"Why, yes," Florence said, smiling. "My sister was born there and my parents called her Parenthope. That's the Greek name for Naples."

"And I'd guess *you* were born in Florence. Am I right?"

"You are right, Mr. Herbert. And were you born in Sydney, Australia?

"No, I'm afraid not." Mr. Herbert laughed. "Although some of my political opponents might say I resemble a kangaroo."

The four people laughed. After making plans to accompany the Herberts to Naples, Florence and Selina returned to their hotel.

"They're awfully nice people," Florence remarked. "I hope we can see them often."

"I'm sure we will," said Selina.

Florence did not know it but she had made as favorable an impression upon Liz and Sidney Herbert as they had made on her. A message arrived the next morning suggesting that all five of them, including Selina's husband, visit Rome's tourist sites together.

"But perhaps I should bow out," suggested Florence. "As couples, you might appear more fashionable."

"Nonsense," Selina exclaimed. "That sounds too much like your mother. I thought you had come with us to escape all those social rituals."

Florence smiled. It did feel good to escape the endless string of formal teas and parties of Lea Hurst and Embly Park. How she wished she could obey her mother and father, enjoying the life they provided her! But something inside her told her this was not the service God had intended.

"All right," Florence answered. "We shall see everything Rome has to offer."

The cheerful quintet did exactly that. Art galleries, museums, parks—none were overlooked. But it was the ceiling of the Sistine Chapel that truly captured Florence's love. The Michelangelo paintings overwhelmed her.

"Please go on," she told the Bracebridges and the Herberts. "I'd like to stay here for a while."

"We're in no hurry," Sidney Herbert replied.

"No, no. I may be here for hours. There's just something about this place. Something so wonderful!"

"I'll stay with you," Selina offered. "We don't want to leave you here alone."

For the next several hours Florence did not speak. Finally she turned to Selina, who was busily writing letters in the pew.

"Do you feel it, Selina? The beauty of this place?" Florence gazed upward, awed by the striking realism of the paintings overhead. "It is like looking into that heaven of angels and prophets."

Selina nodded, attempting to capture the feeling of the close friend beside her. But it was hopeless. Only Florence felt the emotion of the moment.

"I think you should speak with Sidney Herbert about your feelings," Selina whispered. "Share with him. I think the two of you have a common bond."

Florence took Selina's suggestion. After the five English travelers had spent a day visiting the catacombs surrounding Rome, Florence and Sidney found themselves together. The others had gone off for an early supper.

Florence openly shared her personal thoughts. In return, she discovered Sidney understood perfectly.

"We both have money and position," Sidney said.

"We have been raised to know and appreciate the finer things in life. I suppose, by the standards of our society, we should be content with the wonderful benefits we have been given."

"But it isn't enough," Florence injected. "I deeply love my father and mother. I would do nothing to hurt them and bring shame upon the family. Yet something within me calls out. It pulls me."

"And how do you answer this call?"

"I haven't," Florence replied, staring at the floor. "I hope you do not think me foolish, but I sincerely feel God has a special task for me. There is so much misery, so much sickness in the world. Yet we appear to be blind and not see it."

Sidney Herbert leaned back and listened closely to the troubled young woman before him. How clearly he knew and understood! Had he not traveled the same cluttered path of confusion and uncertainty? Finally he raised his hand for Florence to be silent.

"The source of your problem is clear. You wish to be a dutiful, loving daughter and still answer the call of God. At present there seems to be no way to do both." Sidney Herbert paused, aware that Florence was eager to hear every word. "I understand the position you are in. There were those in my own family who wished me to do nothing more than manage the family estates in Wiltshire. A career in government was not respected by many I dearly loved. But sometimes one must listen to the voice beyond the world in which we live. If we pray to God for guidance and direction, we had better be ready to respond."

"Oh, I am!" Florence burst out.

"Do you know what He wants you to do?"

"I believe so. I think he wants me to help the sick, perhaps to become a nurse."

A nurse? Once more Sidney Herbert leaned back

and pondered deeply. A nurse. He had sensed that
Florence's desire for Christian service was deep. But
did she truly realize what path she was considering?

"My dear, I have no doubt as to your sincerity,
but surely you do not grasp what you are suggesting."

"Yes, yes, I know. I have listened to all the ugly
stories."

Sidney shook his head. "They are not stories of
imagination. While I was Secretary of War, I visited
many hospitals. They were prisons of filth and stench.
Patients lay in their beds, praying to die rather than
exist in such conditions."

"Could you do nothing to help them?"

"We made minor improvements, yet there is too
much to be done. Healthy people seldom wish money
spent on those who are sick. As for the nurses, I'm
afraid they were of the worst character. Few were
without bottles of ale hidden in their skirts, not that
I can blame them for trying to endure their pitiful
ordeals."

"But must it always be that way?" Florence asked,
her eyes blazing. "The Lord Himself took such special
interest in the sick. Could the care of those ill and
injured not be a special calling to holy service?"

Sidney Herbert smiled. "You know your Scripture
well, Miss Nightingale. I certainly cannot deny that
the Lord took a special interest in the sick. But you
must not forget that you are a woman, living in a
world that looks with shame upon women in such
work. Should you choose such a direction in your life,
you would expect to suffer much."

Remembering the boredom of countless dances and
parties, Florence slowly shook her head. "There is
boredom in eating a rich pastry or dancing a waltz,
I do believe. I have been bored while surrounded by
one hundred people. Yet I have never felt more

worthwhile than when I have wiped the hot forehead of a sick woman or sat reading to an aged blind man. Those are the times when my life has taken on value and usefulness.''

Sidney Herbert stood up, extending his hand for Florence to rise also. When she did, he took a deep bow.

''You have won me over to your cause, Miss Florence Nightingale. Clearly you have given this matter much thought. Sometimes when you speak, I can hear my own voice echoed from years ago.''

''Then you understand I am not just a foolish girl with silly notions?''

Sidney smiled. ''You are anything but foolish, my dear, and your notions are anything but silly. I have every feeling that you are being directed by the one who guides all who will listen.''

''I hope so,'' Florence murmured. ''I hope so.''

A Visit to Kaiserwerth

Florence dreaded returning to Embley Park. Naturally, there would be many parties to welcome her home—dull, useless parties given by people who were forced to follow the social rules of their class.

"It's not that I am unappreciative," Florence tried to explain, "but it seems so much bother for no reason."

But no one listened. The parties continued.

Before long, Florence was back at her same routine. Her only happy moments were spent reading the book from the German ambassador or visiting with the Herberts.

Liz and Sidney Herbert had become good friends. Florence was overjoyed at being able to help Mr. Herbert with his plans for a new hospital.

"The people of the Pembroke Estates need a place where they can receive good medical attention," Mr. Herbert explained. "Thousands of people live in this area and there is no hospital for them. Would you be interested in helping plan the building?"

"Certainly, I'll be glad to help if I can," answered Florence.

As she did her daily duties, Florence found herself thinking often of Kaiserwerth.

"If only I might find a way to go there," she thought aloud. Finally, her chance came.

"I'm afraid we're going to have to take Parthe somewhere to cure these terrible pains she has been having," Mrs. Nightingale announced. "I think we might all profit from a vacation. We could spend several weeks at the Carlsbad mineral waters and then visit Frankfurt. Germany is lovely this time of year."

Florence's heart jumped with happiness. Frankfurt was only a short distance from Kaiserwerth. While the Nightingale family stayed in Frankfurt, Florence could visit the Kaiserwerth Hospital.

"I think that's a fine idea," Florence agreed. She hurried up the stairs and pulled the treasured book from beneath her bed. She reread every page.

But the vacation plans collapsed.

"I'm afraid we won't be able to visit Germany now," her father explained. "I hear that battles and revolutions are sprouting up all over the continent. Perhaps we can go to the mineral waters at Malvern. It's also a fine resort."

"But isn't there some way we can go to Germany?" Florence pleaded. "I'm not afraid of any revolutions."

"I'm sorry, dear. I can't see what difference it makes where we go for a vacation."

But there was a big difference to Florence. No one else knew of Florence's plan to go to Kaiserwerth. No one else could understand how much she had hoped to go. More and more Florence sensed nursing was part of God's plan for her.

"All that I most wanted to do at Kaiserwerth," she wrote to a friend, "lay for the first time within reach of my mouth, but the ripe plum has dropped.''

Though Mr. Nightingale could not understand the unhappiness of his daughter, he sensed her desire to travel once again.

''Why don't you visit your grandfather in London for a few months, Florence. He would love to see you. You might even enjoy doing some charity teaching in one of the Ragged Schools there.''

Teaching in the Ragged Schools, those schools that tried to reform wayward boys into better citizens. What a wonderful challenge!

''Oh, I'd like to, Father. And perhaps I might visit a few hospitals in the area. Could I, do you suppose?''

Mrs. Nightingale had dropped her sewing to her lap and was about to speak when her husband answered.

''Yes, I think that would be a good idea.''

''Oh, thank you, Father.'' Florence jumped up

from the piano bench and ran upstairs. There would be no time lost in packing.

"But William," Mrs. Nightingale argued after her daughter had left, "you sound as if you're encouraging Florence about those silly notions she has of becoming a nurse. Why did you agree that she could visit the hospitals there?"

"It is time she saw a real hospital. For years she has had that ridiculous plan of becoming a nurse. Yet, she has never seen what nurses are like. Let us give her the chance to visit some hospitals, to see some nurses. After that, I am certain she will cast away some of her foolish dreams."

"I think you are very wise," Mrs. Nightingale observed. "It's time Florence saw for herself just how ugly those hospitals are."

In two days, Florence was off to London. Upon her arrival, she secured a teaching position in one of the schools. She spent any free time she had visiting the local hospitals. The picture was not a pretty one.

Florence soon found that everything her father and mother had said against hospitals and nurses was true. The floors and beds were filthy. There was no systematic procedure for attending the patients. The nurses, many of whom were drinking or sleeping while supposedly working, had no knowledge of tending the sick. More patients died than recovered after entering the public hospitals. But rather than be discouraged at the terrible picture, Florence felt a stronger urge to help.

"There must be some things I can do," she thought. "I must study and learn the finest ways of nursing."

A wonderful opportunity came for Florence when Selina asked her to visit the Mediterranean area.

"This time I *will* visit Kaiserwerth," Florence

announced. "I would like to see how real nurses work."

After seeing the sights in Greece and Egypt, Florence returned through Germany. The night before her trip to Kaiserwerth, she could not sleep. She could not believe she would finally see the place she had read and dreamed so much about.

Pastor Fliedner was waiting for Florence when her carriage jerked to a stop before his house. She was overjoyed when he suggested she remain for a two-week visit.

"And may I work as a nurse?" she asked.

"We work our people here very hard, Miss Nightingale. I am not certain you would enjoy your stay under such conditions."

"Please, Sir. It is what I really want to do."

"All right. After I show you around, we will see that you have a uniform. All of our young ladies wear a blue cotton habit and a white apron. I'm afraid it's not the latest style but—"

"It sounds fine" Florence said.

Kaiserwerth was more than Florence had ever hoped. There was a hundred-bed hospital, a nursery for infants, an orphanage, a small penitentiary, and a school for nurses. Most important, everything was sparkling clean and running in the finest order imaginable.

"Oh, this is beautiful. After seeing the hospitals in England, it is difficult to believe any place like this could exist."

"Why, thank you, Miss Nightingale," Pastor Fliedner said. "We have some dedicated ladies who work very hard."

"I'm sure you do. I only hope I will not be in the way."

"If you're not careful, you'll be in the way of a

snowball. I think I just saw one of our most mischievous lads peek from behind a tree up ahead. He has gained quite a reputation for knocking off the bonnets of any visitors. And I might say, that's a lovely target you are wearing at the moment.''

Florence spotted the youngster about thirty yards away. Just as the pastor had said, he was rolling a fine-packed snowball in his mittens.

''You stay here, Miss Nightingale. I'll—''

''No, please, Pastor Fliedner. If I am to work here, I will have to learn to handle all kinds of situations. I think I might enjoy this one.''

Just as the pastor and Florence neared the point of ambush, the boy raised his arm and sent the snowball whirling. Florence ducked and the missile brushed one of the feathers of her hat. Dashing forward, she grabbed the boy and pulled him to the ground. He thrashed wildly, but could not escape.

''Pastor! Pastor, she's tickling me,'' he said, laughing hysterically. ''Let go of me! Ha, ha! Help, Pastor!''

Pastor Fliedner stood above the two, laughing at the scene.

After several moments, the boy managed to free himself. Covered from head to toe with snow, he raced off, still laughing from the wild ordeal.

Florence brushed some of the snow off as she rose to her feet. She, too, could not stop laughing.

''Miss Nightingale, you did splendidly,'' the pastor announced. ''I'm afraid your dress and bonnet will never be the same, however.''

''Well, Pastor, I believe you mentioned a uniform I would be wearing. I think I will enjoy that more anyway.''

The two weeks at Kaiserwerth seemed to fly by. Florence was busy every minute. The schedule was

a tiring one, but the English visitor never complained.

"We have ten minutes for each of our meals, of which we have four. We get up at five, breakfast at quarter before six," Florence wrote to her mother. "The patients lunch at eleven, the sisters at twelve. We drink tea, that is a drink made from ground rye, between two and three, and sup at seven. Several evenings in the week we gather in the great hall for Bible lessons." All other minutes were spent cleaning, cooking, and helping the sick and orphaned.

As the time approached for Florence to leave, she knew how much she would miss Kaiserwerth. The two weeks had been inspiring. As she closed the door to her room, she noticed someone had taken her suitcases from the hallway.

"Pastor Fliedner, I'm afraid my luggage has disappeared," she said.

"Your luggage has been well taken care of. I believe it is all safely placed in your carriage."

Sure enough, Florence found her suitcases neatly stacked in the carriage.

"But how—"

A loud giggle came from a tree across the road. Florence looked just in time to see a young boy scamper away.

"Why, isn't that the boy who threw the snowball?"

"Yes, it is, Florence. He even asked me when you'd be coming back to visit again."

"Oh, soon, I hope. I want to write a story about Kaiserwerth and all the wonderful things you're doing here. Everyone should know about it."

Florence wrote her story. Within a few months, an anonymous pamphlet was circulating throughout England. It was titled, *The Institution of Kaiserwerth on the Rhine*. Many people, after reading the story, began wondering if something could not be done to improve hospitals and nursing in England. But Florence was not wondering. She knew there could be. And *she* was going to try to do it!

Freedom

"Athe-na! Athe—na. Where are you, you naughty little bird?"

Parthe searched everywhere. Athena, the tiny pet owl Florence had brought home from Greece, seemed to be nowhere in sight.

"Haven't you found that villain yet?" Florence called from upstairs. "I'm beginning to think he has left for good."

"Oh, how can you say that, Flo? I love that bird. Why, she's the nicest little thing we have in this house. If that bird would leave, I think I'd—"

Just then, from her perch on a chandelier, Athena swooped down and whisked off the white cap Parthe had over her hair.

"Help, I'm being attacked! Help!" Parthe's screams echoed through the huge Nightingale house, bringing the servants running.

By the time Parthe had calmed down, all eyes were on Athena, perched on the chandelier and holding tightly to her captured prize.

"That miserable animal!" Parthe shouted. "I hate that little wretch. She could have killed me."

Florence couldn't help but chuckle at her sister. Mr. and Mrs. Nightingale were also smiling.

"But Parthe, weren't you just saying that if that nice little bird left, you'd—"

"Flo, I didn't say any such thing. That bird is the cruelest, meanest—"

"Look," a servant interrupted, "she's coming down."

As everyone watched, the small owl flew to the opposite edge of the sofa from where Parthe was seated. With a proud swaggle, the bird waddled across the sofa and placed the cap in Parthe's lap.

"Oh, isn't that sweet?" Parthe gushed. "That bird has the nicest manners. I think that's the cutest little game she's ever played with me."

"But Parthe, dear. Didn't you just say—"

"Oh, forget what I said." She cuddled the tiny bird to her cheek as the servants, exchanging quiet giggles, returned to their duties.

Seeing an opportunity, Florence asked her mother and father to talk a moment. She had an idea that they must hear.

"I'd like to return to Kaiserwerth," Florence proposed, "and I'd like to study for three months."

"But haven't you given up that foolish notion of nursing?" Mrs. Nightingale scoffed. "Didn't you see how terrible those hospitals were in London?"

"Yes, I did. That's the main reason I would like to go to Kaiserwerth again. I need to study more, and see how Pastor Fliedner managed to establish his fine institutions."

"And I suppose then you'll come back here and do the same thing in England?" Parthe jeered.

"I would like to help, if I can."

"The whole suggestion is ridiculous!" Mrs. Nightingale exclaimed.

"I'm afraid that it isn't, Mother. I've already made my plans to go. I had hoped you would understand that I sincerely want to do this."

Mr. Nightingale had been silent. Parthe and her mother turned to hear what he had to say.

"You sound quite determined, Florence."

"I am, Father."

"But Florence, what will people say?" Mrs. Nightingale could not help but suppose the family name would be totally disgraced.

"If you want to tell people, you may. As for me, I shall be glad to leave without mentioning my destination."

"But surely someone will find out!" Mrs. Nightingale nervously pulled at her lace handkerchief.

"Mother, is it such a terrible thing? I can't understand why it is a disgrace to want to help others."

"But if only you had a chaperone, someone who—"

"Mother!" Parthe exclaimed. "We could go also. We never were able to go to Frankfurt because of the revolutions. Now we could. No one would say anything."

"Yes, Parthe. That is a good plan." Mrs. Nightingale was relieved and breathed easier.

"It still seems very silly for all this bother." Florence marched up to her room, annoyed at the way her family treated her. Finding her diary, she made an important entry.

I am thirty, the age at which Christ began his mission. Now no more childish things, no more vain things, no more love, no more marriage. Now, Lord, let me only think of Thy will.

How wonderful it was to be back at Kaiserwerth!

Pastor Fliedner was happy to welcome Florence again. The little boy who loved to play tricks was now a close friend.

The three months seemed like three days. Florence wrote her mother of the days' activities. ''I find the deepest interest in everything here, and am so well in body and mind. I wish for no other world than this.''

Rising at sunrise each moring, Florence helped dress and feed the children at the Kaiserwerth orphanage. She then went with the deaconesses to the hospital where they cared for the hundred patients. No tasks were too lowly. Often Florence found herself on her knees, scrubbing dirty floors with rough heavy brushes. Pastor Fliedner worried that the work would tire his visitor, who had been raised in comfort and luxury.

''You must rest yourself, Miss Nightingale,'' the kindly pastor admonished. ''The women you work with are peasant women who are accustomed to menial labor.''

Florence looked up as she finished scouring a dusty corner with a wet cloth. ''Pastor, I remember nights when my body ached from dancing at parties. Now it aches each night from the work I have done during the day. I love the aches I have here at Kaiserwerth. Do not take these grand feelings away from me.''

Florence accepted any chore she was given, but she found greatest joy working with the patients. At first, she merely changed their beds and fed them. Soon she was bathing their fragile bodies, combing their hair, and giving them medicine.

But despite her feelings that she was finally doing something worthwhile, Florence sensed there was still more to nursing. Although Kaiserwerth claimed to have a ''school for nurses,'' there were no classes in hygiene, no studies of disease and illness. All that was learned was learned by working directly with the patients.

One night after she had completed her duties, Florence went to Pastor Fliedner's study. Thinking he knew the reason for her visit, the pastor welcomed Florence in.

"You needn't explain why you have come," Pastor Fliedner announced. "I have watched you and know how hard you have been working. You have been doing the work of two women. Yet I knew the strain would tire you. You have served us well, Miss Nightingale, but I free you from any obligation you feel to remain with us."

Florence smiled. "Pastor, I love being here. The work *is* tiring, but it is so useful. I know God has brought me here. What I hope is that you will allow me to do even more."

"More?"

"I have tended the sick and the dying. With my mother, I helped women in childbirth and helped people in their final moments on earth. But I want to observe operations. I want to help those people too."

Pastor Fliedner collapsed in his chair.

"Here I thought you were coming in to say farewell. Now I learn you want to learn and do more. Miss Nightingale, you are a most extraordinary woman."

"I hope you do not think me a nuisance."

The pastor shook his head. "Hardly. Yet I'm not sure you know what you are asking. It is one thing to care for a person with fever and quite another to witness the amputation of a limb."

Florence leaned forward, her jaw set firmly in place. "But a good nurse should be able to help in both situations, I believe. I want to be a good nurse."

"I sense that, my dear. You may have my permission."

Operating methods in 1851 were crude indeed. Patients were strapped to tables so they could not move. Anesthetics to reduce pain or put the patients to sleep were just beginning to find a place in the operating world. There were no antiseptics to prevent infection. Instruments used on one operation were often used on another without being cleaned.

As Florence witnessed her first operation, she almost fainted. The patient's screams were deafening. He tugged and pulled at the table straps. Two men held his arms and legs as the doctor worked.

"Help me, dear Lord," Florence prayed under her breath. She coiled her fingers into tight balls and stiffened her back. Over and over she kept telling herself the operation was necessary to save the patient's life. That thought gave her strength and helped her through the operation.

But with every new experience at Kaiserwerth,

Florence wanted to learn more. Whenever Pastor Fliedner suggested she reduce her work schedule, Florence protested.

"There is so much more I want to know," she insisted. "The training I get one day while I'm here might save a life someday. Please let me go on."

Florence wrote little of the operations she was observing when she wrote to her mother. But when she did share the excitement of witnessing a leg amputation, calling attention to the doctor's calm professional skill, Mrs. Nightingale was not impressed.

"How can you write of such horror, such ugliness?" she wrote back. "Where is the level of decency we instilled within you? You surround yourself with crumpled bones and blood and then write as if you are living in a palace!"

After the three months were over, the return trip to England was an unpleasant one. Mrs. Nightingale and Parthe were so disgusted with Florence they could barely force themselves to speak. They had thought the strain of Kaiserwerth would change Florence, but instead it had strengthened her hopes. Now she would try to find training in a larger location, perhaps a city hospital.

By the summer of 1852, Florence had found the place where she wanted to study. "I would like to go to Paris and train with the Sisters of Charity at the Maison de la Providence," she told her family.

"But you are not a Catholic," her father argued. "Do you know you will be accepted?"

"No, but I shall find out," Florence replied.

After writing Dr. Henry Manning, a leading English Roman Catholic clergyman, Florence was given permission to train with the Sisters of Charity.

"It is a most unusual request you have made," Dr.

Manning wrote, "but you seem to be a most unusual person."

Arriving in Paris, Florence nervously waited to begin her training. The day before she was to start, she learned her grandmother lay dying and had asked for her. Quickly she packed her bags and returned to England.

Following her grandmother's death, Florence retraced her steps to Paris. This time nothing would sway her course. She was determined to learn everything about proper nursing. Somehow she knew this was God's plan.

Each morning she arose and was on her way before dawn. Some days she would visit clinics, while other days she spent in medical libraries.

"What can Flo find interesting in those dull case histories?" Parthe asked herself as she read her sister's letters. "She must be very bored."

Florence was anything but bored. She was too busy filling notebook after notebook with her jottings on each case.

Then, in the spring of 1853, a very special letter arrived from London. Liz Herbert wrote Florence that the Institution for the Care of Sick Gentlewomen in London was looking for a new superintendent. Liz wanted to know if Florence was interested in the position.

Florence couldn't withhold her joy. Here was the chance to apply her nursing knowledge in her own homeland, and here was a chance to practice nursing in a place that would not hurt her family's feelings and reputation. "Gentlewomen" were respected servants of ladies in society. What a wonderful opportunity! Of course she would accept!

Florence bid farewell to Paris, thanking everyone who had helped her. She sailed for England, greatly

excited about her new role as superintendent.

Meeting with her family in London, Florence found them still disappointed with her plans. She decided it would be best if she would find a place to live alone.

As Florence started her new duties, she learned it would not be an easy task. The directors of the home were mostly wealthy women, completely ignorant as to how a hospital should be run. Their ignorance, however, did not force them to be quiet.

"I really don't think it proper for a woman of your class to mingle personally with these lower classes," a haughty matron commented.

"I find it hard to believe that the God who loves us all has divided us by classes," Florence retorted. "And furthermore, I see no reason to open this institution only for Protestants. From now on, this institution shall provide comfort for anyone needing it. We are all God's children."

Behind their backs, Florence laughed at the directors. Though they protested many of Florence's changes, she was constantly showing them the worth of her ideas.

"All patients should have bells they can ring if they need a nurse," Florence suggested.

"But we had no bells before," one of the ladies reminded the new superintendent.

"And perhaps some patients may have died because they could not summon a nurse."

Bells were installed.

"There must be an elevator here," Florence proposed.

"But certainly the nurses can walk from floor to floor without being carried," a woman declared.

"And could *you* walk up and down stairs for twelve hours at a time without collapsing?" Florence retorted.

An elevator was installed.

"This rule forbidding the superintendent to accompany the doctors," Florence pointed out. "What if the doctor is not present when the patient begins to weaken? A superintendent must know what is wrong with the patients for the patients to be treated properly."

The rule was dropped.

Though Florence made enemies of some of the directors, the gentlewomen loved her. Most of them were elderly governesses who had taken ill and been forced to give up their positions. Florence offered them warmth and friendship. After being released, many returned to the hospital to offer their services to the kind woman who had befriended them. Soon the institute was running smoothly under the able direction of the determined Miss Nightingale. Even the most snobbish of the directors had to agree that Florence was efficient.

Florence was happy, too, that her family relationships had mended. Mrs. Nightingale began taking some pride in her daughter's accomplishments, since even the best of London society was chattering about "that fine young lady in charge of the gentlewomen's institution."

One evening, as Florence was making her final rounds, she heard a woman crying. Entering the room, she located the source of the sound.

"Is there something I can do?" Florence asked the old woman who was crying.

"Please, Miss Nightingale. Could you light the candle and stay with me a moment? I'd like to have someone to talk with for a little while."

"Surely, I'll stay as long as you like." Florence lit the candle and pulled a nearby chair close to the bed.

"I hope I didn't disturb anyone," the woman whispered. "I've been so worried about my son. He's decided to become a sailor in the British Navy. Now, with all this talk of war with Russia, I'm afraid he'll decide to go. If anything should happen to him, I wouldn't have anyone left.'' The woman began sobbing.

"You mustn't worry. I guess with all my paperwork here, I haven't been keeping up with the outside news. Why do you think England might go to war?''

"Oh, Miss Nightingale. Haven't you read these?'' The old woman pointed to a pile of newspapers on the table. "Why don't you take them? Perhaps with them gone, I might not worry quite so much.''

"All right. I would like to look them over. Now you get some sleep. I'm certain there is nothing to worry about.''

But later, after reading the newspapers, Florence was not so certain. Russian ships had sunk Turkish ships in the Black Sea. Many men in Parliament were demanding that England stop Russia from trying to take more land.

Florence had a hard time getting to sleep that night.

Call to Arms!

The Crimea. . .

To most English people, the Crimea was merely
a tiny peninsula near Turkey that they had read about
in geography classes. Yet, by the summer of 1854,
many people were closely reading their newspapers
to learn the developments taking place near the
Crimea. The news was gloomy.

The Czar of Russia, Nicholas I, seemed to be asking for battle. Determined to expand his own country, he had ordered his ships to sink all Turkish vessels
in the Black Sea. He then sent Russian troops storm-
ing onto Turkish soil toward the important city of
Constantinople. Russia would control the valuable
waterway called the Bosporus. How simple it would
be to sail Russian ships into the vast Mediterranean
and begin pirating merchant ships.

Both England and France watched the events taking place. At first, they hoped the Turks might prove
too strong for the Russians, but the Czar's forces were
powerful and well-trained. It did not take long for the

English and French governments to see that their trading ships in the Mediterranean were in grave danger unless the conquering Russians could be stopped.

For months, England and France postponed sending troops to fight the Russian forces. Queen Victoria kept hoping that some miracle would stop the Czar's evil plan. Finally, the move was made. English and French troops were sent to the Crimea.

By September, England received wonderful news. The Russians had lost a grueling battle at the Alma River!

From everywhere came outbursts of joy. The proud English had only been at war with the Russians for a short seven months—now the end was in sight.

But joy turned quickly to sadness when the truth of the Alma River Battle was learned. True, England and France had claimed victory at Alma, but not without a heavy toll of dead and injured. Worse than the toll itself was the fact that there were *no* provisions for the wounded soldiers.

"Not only are there not sufficient surgeons, not only are there no dressers and nurses, there is not even linen to make bandages," a war correspondent reported. "No preparation has been made for the commonest surgical operations!"

The British people were outraged.

"Surely there is some mistake," a merchant argued. "The British War Office would have made provisions for our wounded. Perhaps the newspapers are speaking of the French soldiers."

But the newspapers had made no mistake. The British War Office had been trying to save money. They had succeeded—at the cost of many lives.

There was no confusing the treatment of English soldiers with the treatment of French soldiers either.

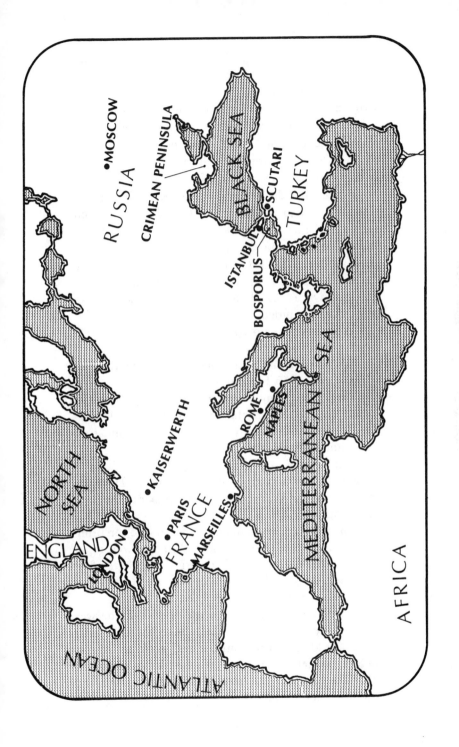

"The French are greatly superior," a correspondent wrote as he compared the handling of the wounded. "Their medical arrangements are extremely good, their surgeons more numerous, and they have also the help of the Sisters of Charity. These devoted women are excellent nurses."

To hear that the French were superior in *anything* was an insult to British pride. It had scarcely been forty years since Britain had heaved its forces against the armies of Napoleon, causing the greedy French commander to go into exile. Now it seemed that the French were winning their own battle against the English by casting shame on the way the British treated its wounded soldiers.

"Why have *we* no surgeons?" an angry British mother demanded to know.

"Why have *we* no Sisters of Charity?" the London Times shouted in headlines.

Florence Nightingale was angry, too. The thought of suffering soldiers at the battlefront weighed heavily on her mind. Finally, she decided she must do something herself.

At the same time, another person in London decided that action must be taken. Sidney Herbert, the Secretary of War, hurled a newspaper to the floor in his office.

"There is one person in this kingdom who can bring great help to those injured boys," he declared to an aide. "Bring me a quill. It's time I wrote a letter. Let us hope that Miss Florence Nightingale will see the tremendous need for her services."

Florence had already seen the need and she was writing a letter, too. She politely asked Mr. Herbert if she could take a few nurses and go to the front. Before her letter had even reached its destination, Florence received one from Mr. Herbert requesting she do exactly that!

"There is but one person in England that I know of who would be capable of organizing and superintending such a scheme," Mr. Herbert wrote. "My question simply is, would you listen to the request to go and superintend the whole thing? You would of course have authority over all the nurses, and I think I could secure you the fullest assistance and cooperation from the medical staff. You would also have an unlimited power to draw on the Government for whatever you thought requisite for the success of your mission," the letter continued.

Florence paused a moment. The idea was almost overpowering. No women nurses had ever been allowed in army hospitals before. Would the doctors and surgeons accept such a change?

"I do not say one word to press you," Mr. Herbert wrote. "You are the only person who can judge for yourself which of conflicting or incompatible duties is the first, or the highest, but I must not conceal from you that I think upon your decision will depend the ultimate success or failure of the plan. Your own personal qualities, your knowledge, your power of administration, and among greater things your rank and position in society give you advantages in such a work which no other person possesses."

Once again, Florence stopped. She wondered if possibly all of the social life she had learned to hate might finally be usable.

"I know that you will come to a wise decision. God grant it may be in accordance with my hopes!" Mr. Herbert concluded.

Florence laid the letter on her desk. So many questions dashed through her mind. What would her family think of her if she accepted? Would they disown her? Could she properly manage the nurses that Mr. Herbert suggested accompany her to the army hospitals? Would she be wise in giving up the fine comfortable conditions she now enjoyed for a mission she knew would be long and difficult?

As she pondered these questions, other scenes came to her mind, scenes of battle, men crying for help, calling for water.

Reaching for a quill, Florence hastily wrote her reply. If she were needed, she would accept! This was truly the service of the Lord!

With the decision made, work for the trip began. Florence hurried to Sidney Herbert's house, which had been selected as the headquarters for interviewing nurses for the trip. As soon as the news spread, two welcome faces appeared at the Herbert home.

"Mother! Parthe!" Florence exclaimed. "How wonderful to see you. I hope you won't scold me for—"

"Scold you? Florence, we've been so proud ever since we heard, we had to come and help. Can you use us?" Mrs. Nightingale carefully rolled up the sleeves of her dress as if to begin scrubbing a floor.

"Oh, this is grand!" Florence cried as she hugged her mother. "We have so much to do before we sail. We can surely put you two to work."

The Herbert house was packed with people. Liz Herbert and Parthe carefully interviewed possible nurses to make the trip. Selina Bracebridge happily told Florence she and her husband were going, too. As soon as she learned this, Florence appointed Selina to help put together uniforms for the nurses. Meanwhile, Florence herself began on lists and charts she must complete.

"How I would like just to set fire to this mound of papers," Florence remarked to Liz. "I had never dreamed all this would be necessary."

"This is a big responsibility, Florence. Haven't you

been reading the papers? Your name is in them all.''

"I haven't even left yet," Florence said with a chuckle. "Perhaps I will be a failure."

"Never!" Liz shot back. "No one will ever call you that—you mark my words."

Locating the right nurses for the trip was no easy task. Though Florence felt she could manage only twenty, Mr. Herbert encouraged her to take forty.

"Forty nurses will not be a burden, Florence. They will all respect your orders. And think how much more can be accomplished."

Florence agreed to take forty.

As the women were interviewed, it became clear that few of them came with the right motives. Word had spread that a nurse making the journey would receive twelve to fourteen shillings a week. The average payment for a working nurse in London hospitals was only seven to ten shillings a week.

"I wish just a few of these women were not interested in money," Selina Bracebridge moaned. Only fourteen of the hundreds who applied were considered suitable. The other nurses would have to come from religious institutions.

On October 21, only four days after receiving Sidney Herbert's letter, Florence led her group aboard a passenger steamer destined for France. She took few things with her, but she kept a small black notebook in her hand. It contained three letters, her most cherished possessions. One was from her mother, wishing her "God's speed on your errand of mercy." The second had come from her old friend, Father Manning, who had helped her get permission to train with the Sisters of Charity in Paris. "God will keep you," he wrote, and told her to seek strength in the "Sacred Heart of the Divine Lord."

The last letter was one from Richard Monckton

Milnes. "God bless you, dear friend," he had written, "wherever you go."

The Nightingale party reached the fishing village of Boulogne at dinnertime. On the shore stood lines of French people, shouting their welcome.

"Come dine with us," a French restaurant owner offered. "My establishment is at your disposal."

"We have a limited budget," Florence explained.

"There will be no payment, Miss Nightingale. It is an honor to have you."

In Paris, too, the nurses were treated as royalty. The French people expressed their warm friendship for the visitors on their way to aid the suffering.

Arriving in Marseilles, Florence announced she would shop for supplies. Selina Bracebridge was surprised.

"But we were told that all necessary supplies were at the Scutari army hospitals," she said. "Why do you want to buy any more?"

"I know, Selina, but we cannot be certain. Those newspaper accounts were very dismal."

"But we were told the newspaper accounts were all false!"

"Can we be certain? Actually, the only thing we can be certain of is that there are many wounded soldiers who need help. We must know that we have the provisions to give it."

Florence's feelings were most fortunate. The nurses would soon learn that the army hospitals were far worse than any newspaper could describe.

Horror at Scutari

"Florence! Florence! The captain says that we will be arriving in a few minutes."

Hearing Selina's call, Florence rose from the bed. The creaking and dilapidated ship, *Vectis*, made sleeping almost impossible. For nine long days the old steamer had crawled across the Mediterranean. Now, the end of the journey was near.

As Florence stumbled to the deck, she saw that a dense fog had developed. The cold rain which had been falling for hours showed no signs of stopping.

"Look! Up there on that hillside!" A nurse's cry turned all eyes to one spot. "Is that the hospital?"

Through the fog, Florence was barely able to see a huge stone building with tall square towers. It seemed to shine a bright gold when occasional rays of sun broke through.

"So we are here," Florence whispered. "Now our work begins. Stay near to us, Lord."

A rowboat pulled alongside the *Vectis* and a rope ladder was quickly lowered. In a moment, a handsome

British officer stood before Miss Nightingale.

"My commander, Lord Raglan, welcomes you and the members of your party, Miss Nightingale," he proclaimed. "He welcomes you on behalf of the entire British Army."

"We are very glad to be here," Florence answered.

"If you will kindly follow me, Miss Nightingale, we shall descend to awaiting rowboats."

"Yes, we will be happy to."

In a few moments, Florence and the nurses were nearing the shore. From each rowboat came the sounds of sneezing and coughing.

"It sounds as if we ourselves need the nursing," Florence remarked. "We shall have to make fast recoveries."

"Oh, Miss Nightingale, when we land don't let there be any red tape delays," an anxious young nurse urged. "Let's get to nursing these poor fellows."

"From all appearances, the strongest will be needed at the washtub," Florence replied grimly.

As the rowboats reached land, the women were helped to shore. Before them stretched a long winding slope.

"I don't suppose there is any other way to reach the hospital?" a woman asked hopefully.

"Afraid not, Ma'am. This is the only way."

Wearily the group trudged up the muddy path. By the time they had reached the hospital, each member of the party was rain-soaked and covered with mud.

"I have a strange feeling that we resemble animals who have been locked out during a rainstorm," Florence observed.

"Miss Nightingale, how can you smile at this?" a voice in the party asked.

"I think we had best find amusement where we can," Florence answered. "We have a lot of work to do here."

The officer showed the women to their quarters, then excused himself. The nurses soon found their new home somewhat inadequate.

"There is no furniture!" a dismayed voice declared.

"Where do we sleep?" someone asked.

"How can forty-four people cook, eat, and sleep in five tiny rooms?"

"There is no fuel for heat!"

"What do we have for food?" still another nurse asked.

All the nurses gradually surrounded Florence. She looked around the quarters and then tried to cheer the group.

"We have come here for one reason," she announced, "to treat the injured. We could hardly expect to live in the queen's palace."

"But Miss Nightingale, we didn't expect *this* either."

"As for me, I find anything a welcome relief after that disgusting old boat we sailed on," Florence said, chuckling.

A few of the nurses smiled in agreement.

"Now we have much to do," Florence continued. "First, we must make this place suitable for living. I think we can start by getting rid of the present occupants—these cockroaches and rats must be removed. There is not room for everyone and though they may have been here first, we must ask them to leave."

Several of the nurses laughed and soon there was a happy spirit midst the busy group. Florence brewed a boiling pot of tea in the hospital below and managed to find some twisted tin cups. The nurses were grateful for the refreshment.

"I might as well tell you what I saw of the hospital," Florence told the assembled nurses later. "We should be happy to have the accommodations we do. The injured soldiers in the rooms below are not so fortunate.''

"But what is it like?'' Selina asked. "Can it be half so bad as the newspaper accounts?''

"Much worse,'' Florence answered sadly. "There are few beds—most of the patients appear to have been left on the floor, without having their uniforms removed. Their shirts are soaked with blood.''

"But how could this be?'' Selina exclaimed. "We were told there were complete provisions and care being given.''

"I know.'' Florence nodded. "We have been greatly misled. Someone has made many serious mistakes. We will have to do all we can to correct them.''

"I think tonight we should get a healthy rest,'' Selina suggested. "Then, tomorrow, we can be up at daybreak, ready to work.''

"I'm afraid we will have a bit of a problem with the doctors also,'' Florence explained. "Dr. Hall, the Chief of the Medical Services here, was furious at the newspaper stories that have been printed about his hospital.''

"But they were all true,'' someone retorted.

"Nonetheless, the doctors have been ordered to ignore us. And there is a rule that no nurse will be allowed to enter a hospital ward unless requested by a doctor.''

"Then how can we do anything at all?'' Selina moaned.

"It's disgusting!'' said one of the nurses. "We have come all this way to help! And now no one will let us.''

"I don't believe we should lose hope,'' Florence said. "If we are patient and show consideration to the doctors, we may win our own battle. Now let us get some sleep.''

By morning, the nurses were aware of a sickening odor. Asked to investigate, Florence returned with more gloomy news.

"All the sewers are clogged below the hospital," she revealed. "The lavatories are useless. The place is filthy and yet there are no scrub brushes or rags."

"It's all so unbelievable," Selina said, shaking her head. "How could any soldier recover under these conditions?"

As the days dragged by, the nurses learned more ugly facts. The tiny portions of meat given each patient were cold. Often, the portion was not meat, but a heavy chunk of gristle. Whatever food was given had to be eaten by hand, for there were no forks, knives, or plates.

"But what if a patient does not have the strength to feed himself?" a nurse questioned.

"Then he does not eat," Florence answered. "At least that is the way it was *before* we came. Now we will help feed those who cannot feed themselves."

Clean sheets and blankets did not exist in the old Scutari hospital. When a monthly washing of materials did take place, clothing and bedding were heaved into a huge bin of cold water and came back from the laundry crawling with lice.

The doctors scoffed at the sight of any of the "Nightingale nurses." Each day, Florence and her helpers would look for the right opportunity to assist.

Finally, on November 6, the right opportunity came.

"Bring the injured in," a surgeon called out. Florence ran to see what was happening. As she stared in disbelief, a narrow trail of stretchers carrying wounded men made its way up the steep slope to the hospital. In the sea, more rowboats, carrying additional injured men, approached the shore.

"But where can you put all these men?" Florence asked the surgeon.

"We'll have to leave them outside the hospital doors," he explained. "There's no room inside."

Florence ran back to her quarters where the nurses were unpacking supplies bought in Marseille. "Hurry," Florence ordered, "we must start packing some bags with straw. Selina, have ten of the women begin sewing sacks. Make them the size of mattresses. Some of you go outside to the horse stables and gather straw. The rest of you start boiling hot tea."

"But will the doctors let us help?" Selina asked.

"I would hope that they could forget their stupid actions and *ask* us to help. I want to be ready—we must be ready!"

All "stupid actions" *were* forgotten, as the sick and injured poured in. Over five hundred new patients joined the already sixteen hundred at Scutari. Miss

Nightingale's party was soon a vital force in aiding the wounded.

"The supplies are low, aren't they?" Florence asked one of the doctors. "We have some from Marseille which we will be glad to offer."

"We have orders not to accept your offers," the embarrassed doctor replied.

"But don't you also have orders to administer help to the best of your ability?" Florence snapped. "We have tried to help. Let us, please!"

"You're right, Miss Nightingale. As for me, you're as fine a nurse as ever I've seen. We'll be happy to accept your supplies."

"Are there more supplies coming?" Florence asked.

"Yes, a ship is right now crossing the Mediterranean on its way here. It is loaded with medical provisions."

But the doctor was mistaken. As he spoke those words, the ship lay at the bottom of the sea, sunk in a vicious hurricane.

By the beginning of December, the Marseille supplies were gone. Something had to be done!

"If supplies are needed, we must have them," Florence told the doctors. "I have funds raised by the British people. With your permission, I shall go to Constantinople and purchase additional necessities. Without your permission, I shall probably do the same thing."

The doctors gave permission—enthusiastically. The walls of prejudice against women nurses were collapsing. Women nurses and male doctors were working side by side for the first time in history.

Florence maintained a twenty-hour day. When she was not administering to the sick, she was furnishing all kinds of supplies.

"I am a dealer in socks, shirts, knives and forks,

wooden spoons, tin baths, tables and forms, cabbages and carrots, operating tables, towels and soap, combs, lice powder, scissors, bedpans and pillows,'' she wrote Sidney Herbert.

One worry still plagued Florence. The hospital now had more supplies and better food, and was better staffed. Yet, there was still the problem of clean laundry for the patients.

''I have it!'' she cried to Selina. ''We shall open a laundry in Scutari village. We can set up some boilers, pay some of the women in the village to work, and the hospital patients will have clean shirts and sheets.''

''But will it work?'' Selina wondered.

''Anything will be better than ignoring the situation as we have done this far,'' Florence answered.

The plan did work. Within weeks, wounded men slipped into clean hospital shirts and snuggled between clean bed linens.

"Am I in heaven?" one soldier asked a nurse as he climbed into a clean bed.

December brought cold winds—and more and more wounded men. Rooms were cramped for space so that a nurse could not even walk between patients.

Florence told one of the chief doctors, "More room must be found!"

"We will have to make do," the doctor replied.

"Dr. McGregor, there is space nearby for another thousand men. We must add to the hospital," Florence argued.

"Who could pay for the workmen?" Dr. McGregor asked sharply.

"Sidney Herbert has told me to spend anything necessary. I shall write to Lord Stratford, who has been given personal charge of the expenses."

Florence wrote to Lord Stratford. He approved the project and sent his wife to assist. The workmen began constructing the addition, but one day, without warning they decided to strike. Florence relayed the news to Lord Stratford. He answered by saying he knew nothing about the idea. Puzzled and angry, Florence hired more workmen to finish the job. It was completed just in time for a new surge of wounded men from the battlefront.

"But you had to use your own money for much of that project," Selina protested to Florence.

"There was a need," Florence replied. "Anyway, if I recall Scripture correctly, Matthew tells us, 'Where your treasure is, there will your heart be also.' Whatever money I possess, I would gladly give to have these poor men healthy and home."

Unwanted Guests

Slowly, ever so slowly, Florence began to break down the walls of resentment the army doctors had against her nurses. Although she firmly kept charge of her people, she never raised her voice. In her letters back to England, she affectionately referred to the doctors as "Bears" and the orderlies as "Cubs."

Still the injured poured in. Beds inside the Barracks Hospital at Scutari stretched for four miles, with eighteen inches between the beds.

"These poor fellows bear pain and mutilation with an unshrinking heroism which is really superhuman," wrote Florence, "and die, or are cut up, without a complaint."

Although Florence heard few complaints from her patients, the nurses she commanded were not so silent. One woman she had to send home shortly after their arrival. Soon four more rebelled against her strict orders and demanded to leave.

"No one shall force you into remaining," Florence told the disgruntled nurses, "but surely you can see the need for your services here."

"We cannot understand your objection to a swig or two of ale now and then," their bold leader declared. "You bring us to this wretched, filthy place and then expect us to work like beasts. How can *you* stand the stench and ugliness?"

Florence's eyes blazed. "One works to improve what can be improved."

"But we find a sip of ale helps remove that which has not yet been improved."

"There will be no drinking among my nurses," Florence announced with renewed force. "I thank you for what you have done while you were here. I shall assist with your departure in any way I can."

One morning, as Florence wiped the feverish head of a young man who had had his arm amputated the day before, one of Florence's nurses approached. Mrs. Roberts beckoned Florence away.

"What is it?" Florence asked.

"I just overheard one of the Medical Heads, Miss Nightingale. He was saying there are more nurses coming here from England. Over forty of them, the physician says, with no training at all."

Florence could not believe her ears.

"You must have misunderstood, Mrs. Roberts. I have a written promise from Mr. Sidney Herbert that no additional nurses will be sent here until I request them."

"I only know what I heard, Miss Nightingale. I knew you would want to be informed."

Florence's thoughts were spinning inside her head. There was no housing for more nurses, no food either. Now, when Florence and her own nurses were beginning to gain respect and assistance—no, it had to be a mistake, a rumor.

Florence learned that it was true. Forty-six women, led by an old friend, Mary Stanley, would soon arrive at Scutari. To make matters worse, the visitors were not even put under Florence's supervision. The party was assigned to Dr. William Cummings, a senior medical officer.

"Why, dear God? Am I such a failure in the eyes of the people back home?" Florence asked. She fought to control her anger, remembering Matthew's warning in 5:22: "Whoever is angry with his brother without a cause shall be in danger of the judgment."

"But I do have 'cause'," Florence told herself. "I have good 'cause' to be angry." Quickly she took her pen and wrote to Sidney Herbert.

Dear Mr. Herbert,

When I came out here as your Supt. it was with the distinct understanding (expressed both in your own hand writing and in the printed announcement which you put in the Morning Chronicle which is here in everyone's hands) that nurses were to be sent out at my requisition only, which was to be made only with the approbation of the Medical Officers here. You came to me in great distress and told me you were unable for the moment to find any other person for the office and that, if I failed you, the scheme would fail.

I sacrificed my own judgment and went out with forty females, well knowing that half that number would be more efficient and less trouble, and that the difficulty of inducing forty untrained women, in so extraordinary a position as this (turned loose among 3000 men) to observe any order or even any of the directions of the medical men, would be Herculean.

Experience has justified my foreboding. But I have toiled my way into the confidence of the medical men. I have, by incessant vigilance, day and night, introduced something like order into the disorderly operations of these women. And the plan may be said to have succeeded in some measure, as it stands . . .

> At this point of affairs arrives at no one's requisition, a fresh batch of women, raising our number to eighty-four . . .
>
> The quartering them here is a physical impossibility, the employing them a moral impossibility.

Florence stopped for a moment. She fought against tears, biting her lip to bring on a stinging pain that would help her continue.

> You must feel I ought to resign, where conditions are imposed on me which render the object for which I am employed unattainable . . . You will appoint a Superintendent in my place until which time I will continue to discharge its duties as well as I can.
> Believe me, dear Mr. Herbert,
>
> > Yours very truly,
> > Florence Nightingale

There was no stopping the tears now. Florence set the pen down, wiping her wet cheeks with her dress cuff. How Mother would disapprove of such an action, Florence thought suddenly. The silly notion brought a quick smile to Florence's lips.

It was a fleeting smile however, and the only one Florence would have about the entire incident. When the Stanley party arrived in Constantinople on December 15, 1854, Florence sent Mrs. Bracebridge to their ship.

"You must not disembark," Selina told the newcomers. "There is absolutely no place for you to stay in Scutari."

"Can we not stay with Miss Nightingale?" Mary Stanley asked.

Selina shook her head. "Miss Nightingale's quarters are now accommodating forty people in space adequate for three. There is no food, water, or fuel for you."

Mary Stanley's face reddened. Her eyes squinted in rage.

"We shall not bother Miss Nightingale," she declared. "We shall make Dr. Cummings aware of our arrival. He shall look after us."

"I hope that he will," Selina Bracebridge answered.

Once notified, Dr. Cummings wanted nothing to do with the party of nurses. He had barely learned to tolerate Florence and her helpers. The thought of welcoming more "untrained troublemakers" into the Scutari hospitals horrified Dr. Cummings.

Again Mary Stanley and her women appealed to Florence for help.

"We cannot go back even if we wanted to," Miss Stanley admitted. "We have no money."

Florence raised her eyebrows in surprise. "But I understand you left England with fifteen hundred pounds sterling!"

"Ladies in my party cannot be expected to travel as peasants," Mary Stanley snapped back.

"Nor would I expect each of you to travel like the queen herself!" Florence countered. "You seem to look on this entire excursion as some vacation. We are fighting a war here, Miss Stanley. Men and boys are dying."

For the first time Mary Stanley seemed to lose her forcefulness. Florence felt a twinge of sympathy.

"I shall loan you ninety pounds sterling from my own income," she said softly. "This will be spent on your immediate necessities. If more is needed, I shall see to it."

Reluctantly Mary Stanley accepted.

Early in January of 1855, Florence received a letter from Sidney Herbert. He apologized for the Stanley party and accepted full responsibility. He put her in complete control, begged her not to resign, and offered to pay the expenses of the Stanley party returning to England.

"Mr. Herbert probably does not know how these women travel," Florence laughingly told Selina Bracebridge.

"Are you going to forgive him?"

Florence thought for a moment. "It is not an easy thing to overlook. The entire situation has upset me greatly. I shall give it serious consideration."

None of the other nurses or the injured soldiers were allowed to know the hurt that Florence carried. Selina Bracebridge was sworn to secrecy and would not share her secret.

A personal letter from Queen Victoria boosted Florence's feelings. Her Highness asked for more direct information about her British soldiers, declaring that "no one takes a warmer interest or feels for their sufferings or admires their courage or heroism more than their Queen. Day and night she thinks of her beloved troops."

It was a touching letter, one which moved Florence deeply. Queen Victoria sent small gifts to the soldiers and asked that Florence distribute them. Her Majesty asked Florence if there was any personal request she desired.

There was no need to ask twice. According to British war rules, a soldier injured in action had his pay reduced four and a half pence a day. A soldier becoming sick while in active service lost twice that amount.

"The stoppage should be the same for sickness as for wounds," Florence wrote Queen Victoria. "Both illness and injury result from the men being here in service to their country."

The rule was changed immediately.

To resign or not to resign? Florence weighed the decision carefully. It did not help the situation when Mary Stanley came to Florence and requested more money. Yet she gave her more, three hundred pounds from her own purse.

But it was the words of Matthew 18:21 and 22 in the Bible that brought Florence to her final decision. By candlelight, she was paging through the worn volume when she saw the passage.

"Then came Peter to him, and said, Lord, how oft shall my brother sin against me, and I forgive him? till seven times? Jesus saith unto him, I say not unto thee, Until seven times: but, Until seventy times seven."

The words spoke clearly to her. And if Matthew did not speak with eloquence enough, there was always Luke 17:3. "If thy brother trespass against thee, rebuke him; and if he repent, forgive him."

Florence closed the Bible, lay back, and closed her eyes. "How clearly You give us direction, dear Lord, if we will only stop to listen."

Florence washed her hands of the entire Mary Stanley situation. The forty-six women persuaded different Medical Officers to allow them to go to various hospitals. Eleven headed to Balaclava, five were accepted at Scutari, and Mary Stanley led a group to Koulali. Three went home immediately, claiming, "The ugliness and filth are more than we can accept."

In March, Mary Stanley returned to England. The strain had tired her "beyond endurance."

But Florence endured. Often she was on her feet for twenty-four hours at a time. She was known to stand for eight hours dressing wounds. When her weary legs gave way, she continued on her knees.

"No soldier shall ever die alone," she told her nurses. "If you are too tired, call me to the bedside and I shall stay with him until the end."

Florence meant what she said. During the winter of 1855 and 1856, she witnessed over two thousand deaths. She prayed constantly for strength. And when a patient died, a final duty remained.

                                Barracks Hospital
                                        Scutari
Mr. Sanderson,
    It is with the most sincere sorrow & sympathy, that I am compelled to send you sad news of your Son, George Sanderson, I.T.C.
    He came into this Hospital on Monday last, the 3rd of March, ill with Diarrhea. He grew gradually worse till this morning, when, I grieve to say, that at 8 o'clock, he breathed his last. I hope it may be some consolation to you in this sad event, to know that he received every care & attention during his last illness in this Hospital. He had the constant care of the Doctors of the Hospital, & of the Nurse who attended in his ward. The Chaplain of the Hospital who attended regularly in his ward, to read to the patients & pray with them—all that he could take in the way of nourishment was given to him.
    The night before his death, he expressed a desire that 2 pounds 4 which he had with him, should be sent to you. I have it in my care, & I will send it to you by the next Post.
                        With sincere sympathy for your
                        great loss I remain yours truly
                            Florence Nightingale

    Often the tears filled Florence's eyes as she wrote such letters. She tried to make each one as personal as possible.
    "Please, Lord, help me in this mission," she whispered.
    The help was always there.

"The Lady of the Lamp"

Winter was cruel to Scutari. The worn hospital shook with wintry blasts. The Nightingale nurses often had to stop their nursing in order to patch up holes which were letting in a freezing wind.

Each day Florence would supervise the nurses in the wards. The menus were checked, dressings on the wounds changed, conferences with the doctors held—all while wearing a happy smile for the patients.

"Good morning, Miss Nightingale," the patients would greet her. They seemed to live for the few moments she would spend with them. But with twelve thousand soldiers packed into the hospitals of Scutari, those moments were very short.

"How does she do it?" a nurse asked Selina Bracebridge. "She's up before dawn making the rounds of the wards. Still, I see her light burning long into the night. It's almost unbelievable! The Lord surely must give her strength."

"She's an unbelievable woman," Selina replied, "one of the Lord's special servants."

Her usual day's work would have exhausted the average woman. Not Florence! After the sun had gone down, she went to her room and wrote reports to send back to Sidney Herbert. Although he asked for brief reports, he got much more. Florence devised speedier methods of buying supplies, plans for reorganizing hospitals, suggestions for training better nurses, and a system of keeping hospital records.

As if it were not enough to supervise her staff and complete her reports, Florence had still another duty. She had to keep her nurses happy. This was not always easy.

"Miss Nightingale, I know you're busy, but—"

"I always have time to speak with one of my best nurses. What can I do for you, Mrs. Lawfield?" Florence closed her books and looked up at the nurse standing before the desk.

"Well, I came out here ready to submit to everything and be put upon in every way. I've tried to be cheery about each thing and everything, but there is a limit to what one can tolerate."

Florence could see Mrs. Lawfield was most upset. "You've been doing a fine job," Florence offered. "What seems to be upsetting you?"

"Well. Well," Mrs. Lawfield fidgeted, "it's these caps we have to wear, Miss Nightingale! They suit one face, but they don't suit others. They certainly don't suit mine. If I'd known about having to wear these headpieces, I probably wouldn't have agreed to come."

"Oh, Mrs. Lawfield, it would have been most difficult without you." Florence glanced at the uniform Mrs. Lawfield was wearing. True, it was drab. There had been so little time to make the uniforms. The gray tweed gown wrapped around Mrs. Lawfield tightly, while the closefitting cap perched on her head.

"I suppose it sounds silly to you, Miss Nightingale. I know you have so much to do that I hated to—"

"One of the most important things I have to do is watch out for the welfare and comfort of my nurses," Florence declared. "If you feel the cap makes you a poorer nurse, then please do not wear it."

"Oh, Miss Nightingale, I'm sure it doesn't affect my work. I had just thought—" Mrs. Lawfield stopped in the middle of what she was saying. "I had just thought, oh, I'm being silly. Please excuse me for taking up your time." Mrs. Lawfield gave her cap a light tap and walked away. Florence couldn't help but smile.

The most satisfying moments for Florence were with the patients. The comfort she brought was unmeasurable.

One night, as Florence carried her trusty lantern for a final check on one of the wards, she heard a weak voice calling her name. As she followed the sound of the call, her light shone down on a crying young transport sailor. His leg had been badly shattered and the pain was unbearable. Florence knew that he would be operated on in the morning. There was little hope the leg could be saved.

"Miss Nightingale, might I have a drink of water?"

"Surely." She walked to a nearby bedstand and returned with a cool glassful. "This will refresh you."

As she poured the water into his burning mouth, Florence gently stroked his forehead. Her hand was soothing and cool.

"Miss Nightingale, are they going to take my leg off?" The tone of the sailor's voice clearly showed it required great courage to ask.

"I don't know for certain, William," Florence answered softly. "But there is one thing I know. I shall be here all the time. I know they will save your leg if possible. And I can tell you will be a fine and brave sailor about it.''

''I'm really not ver-y br—brave,'' the boy whimpered.

''I hate to say you are wrong, William, but I have seen many soldiers in this hospital. I can truthfully say that you are one of the bravest.'' Florence stood and turned to go.

''You wouldn't try and fool me, Miss Nightingale. My mother always used to give me a compliment when she wanted me to do a piece of work.''

''That's a rather wise method,'' Florence murmured. ''But I'm afraid in this case I am being completely honest with you. Now go to sleep. God keep you safe.''

The sailor watched the lantern as it moved across the room. Occasionally it paused at a bedside, then moved on. Finally as it disappeared in the darkness, the sailor fell back on his pillow.

''I can't wait to write mother about this,'' he said to himself. ''Florence Nightingale sayin' I was one of the bravest here.''

Florence's charm with the patients did not stop with the soldiers. Another patient, a bubbling young drummer orphan named Tommy, declared he was ''Miss Nightingale's man.''

''I'm givin' up my drums to serve a new commander,'' he announced. ''Miss Nightingale is givin' the orders from now on.''

As soon as he could walk, Tommy showed he was not just pretending. He ran errands, swept the floors, and polished Florence's lantern until he could see his own face. Sometimes he even persuaded the busy Miss Nightingale to sit down and relax for a few minutes.

''You've got to rest more,'' he'd scold. ''You run around this place like you were a work horse. You're

always tellin' everybody else to rest, yet you don't ever."

But Florence's rests were few. Each time a problem would be solved, another would sprout. From England came complaints that there were too many Roman Catholic nuns serving as nurses.

"So few of the injured are Roman Catholics. Why should there be so many Roman Catholic nuns attending them," some English newspapers asked. "Surely they will try to gain converts."

Such stories angered Florence.

"It is ridiculous to think that these nuns are seeking converts in these hospitals," Florence protested. "They are like the rest of us, interested in bringing aid and comfort to the injured soldiers."

Still the rumors spread. Some claimed Miss Nightingale was a "secret agent for Rome." Florence became so irritated that she decided to ignore the controversy and offer no further comments. Gradually, the issue died down.

In early May, Florence sailed on board the *Robert Lowe*. Her destination was Balaclava.

"I only hope Dr. Hall will see that the women can do a great amount of good," Florence told Selina Bracebridge. "It is most difficult for some men to accept a woman who does *anything* except cook and sew."

"Let us hope he will welcome your visit," Selina said. "Some of the doctors back at the hospital have hinted that Dr. Hall is quite set in his ways."

"And *upset* at mine," Florence said, smiling.

When the ship docked at Balaclava, Dr. Hall was not among the welcoming greeters.

Yet, as she left the ship, Florence was immediately surrounded by a group of government officials and British officers. Tommy was flabbergasted.

"I've never seen so many medals!" he said.

At her request, Florence was granted permission to visit the front lines of battle. A thoroughbred mare with a shiny side-saddle was brought to her for the trip.

For hours, Florence rode close to the battlefront. As she inspected some of the hospitals, she knew there was much dislike for her presence. Dr. Hall had once again ordered the medical staff, including the nurses, to ignore Florence. Her suggestions for improving hospital routine were met by stern and hostile stares.

"Dr. Hall has done a fine job of turning everyone here against me," Florence told Selina. "The only friendly faces I see in the hospitals are those of the patients. Occasionally a nurse looks a bit sheepish, but they know that if they disobey Dr. Hall's orders, they won't be allowed to nurse. I can hardly blame them."

But the hospital patients had no orders from Dr.

Hall. The stories of the wonderful "Lady of the Lamp" had crossed the countryside. Everyone knew her—everyone loved her.

When Florence returned from an afternoon of hospital inspections one day, she collapsed in a chair. How tired she felt! And the room was so hot.

"Tommy," she called. "Selina, could you come here a moment?"

As they hurried into the room, the drummer boy and Selina knew something was wrong.

"I've got to send for a doctor, Florence," Selina announced.

"Don't be ridiculous. If you'd just help me to bed—" But as Florence tried to stand, she fell back into the chair. A sudden weakness had stolen her strength.

That night, several doctors hovered over Florence's bedside, as she had so often done to others. Their faces were grim as they announced the results of their examinations.

"It's a severe case of Crimean fever," one of the doctors said quietly. "She's very near death."

As word of Florence's illness spread back to Scutari, the wounded soldiers turned to the wall and cried. When people in London heard the news, they turned pale with grief.

"She can't die," everyone prayed. "She just can't."

Tommy, "Miss Nightingale's man," sat by her bedside unable to move. He couldn't take his eyes off the sleeping face of the kind woman who had befriended him.

Lord Raglan, the commander of the British military forces, made a special trip to visit the woman who had helped his men.

"The queen sent word for me to pay you a call,"

Lord Raglan explained, "and I had already planned to come anyway."

"You are very kind," Florence whispered weakly.

"One of your doctors has told me you are making a fine recovery. Her Majesty will be delighted at the news, as will all of my men."

"I will be glad when I can return to my work," Florence answered.

"But you must not worry yourself, Miss Nightingale. You need a great deal of rest. When do you plan to return to England to rest?"

"That will depend on you, Lord Raglan. Whenever the fighting is over and there is no more work to be done here, I will go back to England. By now, people in England have probably forgotten all about me."

But Florence was wrong. The letters sent home by the soldiers had made Florence a national heroine. Everywhere, people spoke with glowing praise of the wonderful Florence Nightingale.

"England has two queens now," a newspaper proclaimed. "There's Her Majesty Queen Victoria and Her Royal Highness Florence Nightingale."

People had grown to love the courageous young woman who had given up her rich and comfortable life in order to help the soldiers at the Crimean battlefront. In almost every home was a picture or statue of Florence. Songs were written and sung about "The Nightingale in the East." Newly built ships were christened and village streets were named in her honor. And child after child was lovingly called "Florence" by proud new parents.

The English people at home were overjoyed at the news of Florence's recovery. Word traveled fast and many happy faces gathered at parties to celebrate.

"*She's* our finest soldier!" a smiling innkeeper cheered. "They don't come any better than Miss Nightingale."

"She should get a medal," someone declared. "She should get every medal!"

"She wouldn't want any medals," the innkeeper argued. "But we should certainly give her something."

Everyone agreed. Florence Nightingale should be rewarded.

On November 29, 1855, a huge meeting was held in London. From all parts of England came royalty, politicians, and peasants. Florence was loved by all—both rich and poor. After several hours of wonderful speeches, Sidney Herbert rose and made an important statement. A Nightingale Fund would be started to raise money for a nursing school.

When Florence received a letter from Sidney Herbert, she was pleased. Still, she had little time to think about planning a nursing school. There was a war going on—and there were injured soldiers who needed care.

The soldiers, however, learned about the Nightingale Fund. Among them, they gladly pledged over $45,000.

"It's the best way we can find to help repay a little of what she's done for us," a soldier remarked.

It finally became clear that the war was coming to an end. Still Florence kept working her exhausting schedule. She set up reading rooms in the Scutari hospitals. Thousands of books were sent from England. Seeing that the reading rooms were so successful, Florence decided to open night classes for soldiers. Shortly after she had sent her suggestion to England, two schoolmasters and two thousand books arrived. Some of the men who had never attended school were now doing homework!

At last, on March 30, 1856, a peace treaty was

signed with Russia. The Crimean War was over! It was time to go home.

Final Chores

Peace.

Home.

It is amazing how certain words carry a gentle, loving tone. Love. Family. Lord. Jesus. Florence mused over the melodic musical lilt the words carried as she made her way among the countless hospital beds at the General Hospital in Balaclava. What a strange contrast those words made with others which can grow so tiresome and ugly!

War.

Hate.

Anger.

Yes, those words carried their own message too. How harsh that message sounded! Surely people could sense the joyful song the Lord wished for those who loved Him.

"Miss Nightingale? Is that you, Miss Nightingale?"

The voice of a patient in a nearby bed brought Florence out of her thinking. Quickly she hurried to the soldier in his bunk.

"Yes, son, I am here."

"Ma'm, is it a good day out? I haven't seen the sun shine in so long I've almost forgotten what it looks like."

Florence shook her head. "You won't be seeing it today either, I'm afraid. Even my old trusty parasol has sprung a few leaks in it."

The soldier smiled. "My mum has a parasol like yours. I gave it to her as a gift one time. She never uses it though. Says it's too fine to carry out in the rain."

"Might just be too fine because it came from you," Florence said, pulling up the blanket at the foot of the bed. "Loved ones hold things dear that way."

"Um-m, maybe," the boy whispered, gazing at the parasol Florence had leaned against the bed.

Suddenly Florence had an idea. "Say, I have a favor to ask of you," she said.

"Of me? I-I really can't do much."

"Well, perhaps I shouldn't be bothering you with such a silly notion, but I will anyway. My quarters are so cramped—I barely have room to turn around. I was just hoping you might keep an eye on this parasol for me. Even if I could just slide it under your bed—"

"Oh, no, Miss Nightingale. Here, let me have it. I'll keep it right beside me."

"If it's any bother—"

The soldier shook his head, gently holding the parasol on the blanket. "Oh, no. No trouble. It's—I know it sounds foolish—but it's almost like having a bit of Mum and the home right here."

"Why, I never thought of it quite that way," Florence lied. "Well, take good care of it. I'll probably be needing it again the way it's been raining here every day."

When it wasn't raining at Balaclava, it was snow-ing. Florence and the three-nurse team she had brought from Scutari quickly worked to clean the General Hospital. It took them two full days to carry the dirt and trash from the building, and another three days to treat the bedsores of the patients.

Florence gave little thought to the parasol she had loaned away until late one night when she was doing rounds. A noise from an upper rafter attracted her attention. At first she thought rain might be dripping from the ceiling. But no, it was not water dripping. She saw movement.

Florence held her lamp high. Still she could not see anything. Only the rustling sound continued.

"You best not get any closer, Miss Nightingale."

The voice startled Florence. She hadn't realized that anyone nearby was awake.

"But you do hear that sound?" she murmured. "It's coming from one of the rafters."

"It was there last night too, ma'm. I think it could be a rat."

A rat! How many rats were there in this war? Ever since arriving from England, Florence had been kill-ing rats. Why did these ugly creatures hide in hospitals?

Again the noise came from above. Yes, it did sound like footsteps. Small, scurrying footsteps.

Florence glanced around quickly. She gripped her lamp even tighter, feeling a bit safer with something in her hand. Across the floor she saw the young soldier with whom she had left her parasol. She hurried to it.

"If there's a rat up there now," she said, "he won't be there long."

Florence took the parasol from where it lay on the bed. She felt a hand cover hers.

"Ma'm, you best be careful. Those are mean creatures."

Florence nodded. "There are many battles to be fought out here," she whispered. "You have fought yours with courage. It is the example we all must follow."

Florence carried her lamp to a small tablestand. Setting it down, she strained to hear any sounds overhead. Yes, there they were again. Small scratching noises, soft and quick.

Some distance away Florence spotted an old chair. She hurried to it, picked it up, and returned. She pushed the chair against the wall, immediately beneath the sounds.

"Lord, please be with me," she murmured, hoisting her skirts slightly so as to climb upon the chair. The parasol felt wet in her clenched hand and she realized how she was sweating.

Staring into the side rafters between the wall and the ceiling, Florence squinted. The light from her lamp cast eerie shadows. Moans from a few soldiers lying in pain broke the silence of the night.

Florence's pulse quickened. She found herself staring at two smaller pools of light. A rat! No small mouse shape, this one. More like a good-sized cat, well-fed from countless pilfered meals. The creature cringed back at first, apparently caught off guard by Florence. Then the ugly rodent snapped forward a bit, like a snake readying its leap.

Almost losing her balance, Florence quickly fumbled to regain her footing. Clutching the parasol as tightly as she could, she swung the weapon hard against the rat. It connected harshly, stunning the vicious creature.

"You all right, Ma'm?" a patient called from below.

"What did you hit?" asked another voice.

But Florence had no time for conversation. The

enemy was merely dazed and could easily strike out. A flicker of candlelight caught the bright gleaming teeth of the rat. Spittle dripped from its mouth; its eyes blazed with anger.

"Down with you!" Florence burst out again, once more pounding the parasol against the rat's head.

This time the weapon hit home. It cracked against the beast's head. Fatally injured, the rat dropped to the floor below.

Florence descended her chair to the cheering of the nearby patients. Her heart still thumped loudly as she stood for a moment to catch her breath.

"You should have commanded our battalion!" a patient called out.

"Three cheers for Miss Nightingale!" another shouted.

And as Florence hurried off to find a box for the dead rat, the hospital echoed with loud cheering and applause.

Each day found more soldiers heading home. Letters from Parthe and Mrs. Nightingale arrived, begging Florence to leave the battlefront and "hasten back to England where you belong."

"There are still tasks remaining here," Florence wrote back. "But I do long for the warmth and love of you all."

Much like a captain remaining with his ship, Florence felt the call of duty to visit each British hospital to make sure it was properly closed. Her arrival at the Land Transport Hospital left her shocked and horrified. Despite official orders carried to every military hospital the year before, it appeared none had reached this location. Conditions had not changed, and patients suffered from poorly cooked and inadequate rations, exposure, frostbite, insanitary disposal of waste—all that Florence had insisted be corrected.

"Everything is just where it was eighteen months ago," she wrote to Sidney Herbert. "There is still so much to be changed."

From hospital to hospital Florence traveled, never leaving until she was sure someone was in charge who would tend to improvements. Heavy snowfalls failed to slow her pace or spirit. Roadways became slick and dangerous. She rode in a mule cart with one driver.

One night, as heavy snowflakes drifted from the sky, the cart skidded to one side. Ambrose, the driver, warned against continuing.

"You'd not like to be lying in one of those hospital beds yourself, would you, Miss Nightingale?"

"I have complete faith in your handling of the reins, Mr. Hilton. We *must* continue. Surely a mite of snow would not hinder your abilities."

Ambrose Hilton shook his head. He knew better than to make an argument. When Florence Nightingale decided, it was a decision that could not be swayed.

Slivers of sleet speckled the cold night air. Florence lifted the wool scarf around her neck. Suddenly the cart slid to the side, then back. The two mules pulling the vehicle could not hold their footing on the glassy ice.

"Hold on, Miss Nightin—"

Before Ambrose could finish his warning, the cart toppled over. Florence sprawled to the right side, the driver rolling over her. In the moonlight, the mules struggled to their feet. But the cart hitch was broken.

"Are you all right, Miss Nightingale?"

Florence lifted herself in the snowbank, stretching her arms and legs. "I believe I am physically unhurt, Mr. Hilton. But I confess that I feel a bit foolish. It is one thing to be steadfast in work, yet it is quite another to be foolhardy. You would not presume to tell me how to nurse in a hospital. I would have done well to heed your suggestion in driving this mule cart. I apologize, Mr. Hilton.''

Fortunately, only Florence's pride was hurt. As she and her driver walked the remaining two miles to the hospital, she promised to listen a bit more carefully to those around her.

The next afternoon, while Florence was visiting patients in the Monastery Hospital, she was surprised to see Ambrose coming toward her. The man was smiling.

''Colonel McMurdo heard of our accident last evening,'' Ambrose said. ''He has already provided another vehicle for your use.''

Florence was speechless. She hardly expected action so quickly. Now if only the Army could be so efficient in more important matters!

Outside, Florence circled the hooded baggage cart which had been ordered for her transportation. It was larger than the mule cart and appeared to be sturdier as well.

''The cover will keep out some of the rain and snow,'' Ambrose observed. ''Wheels are stronger too.''

Florence nodded. ''This time I'll listen to what you say, Mr. Hilton. If you consider the carriage a sound vehicle, I shall ride in it without fear.''

As her driver, Ambrose Hilton became Florence's good friend. Another ally in the final months at the battle areas was Alexis Soyer. From meager army rations, Soyer seemed able to produce magnificent banquets.

''Others,'' Florence wrote home, ''have studied cookery for the purpose of gormandizing, some for show. But none except he for the purpose of cooking large quantities of food in the most nutritive and economical manner for great quantities of people."

Not everyone in the army hospitals welcomed Soyer upon his arrival. Medical officers treated the chef coolly, having little use for the fat, short fellow. But Florence encouraged her nurses to treat Soyer kindly.

"It is the First Book of Samuel of Scripture which tells us, 'Man looketh on the outward appearance, but the Lord looketh on the heart.' If the doctors we serve wish to shun Mister Soyer because they do not appreciate his appearance, that is their concern. We shall help him in any way we can."

The advice proved fruitful. Soyer appreciated Florence and her helpers. "You care for the injuries and illnesses of your patients," he declared, "and I shall fill their insides with the best stuffing I can."

"A worthy exchange," Florence agreed.

Soyer kept his promise. He discontinued the process of boiling every food until all flavor was gone. He made up new recipes for soup and stews. No problem seemed too big for him.

"We have no ovens for baking fresh bread and biscuits," his assistants complained. "Yet that is what you tell us the patients need."

Soyer shook his head. "We shall invent and build new ovens."

The creative chef did exactly that. He also invented a Scutari teapot which made and kept hot tea for fifty men at one time. To other hospitals he sent framed parchment copies of his favorite recipes. Always wanting to get the most from everyone, Florence approached Soyer with another suggestion.

"You clearly display rare talents in the kitchen," she told him one evening as she enjoyed a cup of his hot tea. "I wonder if a man can teach others such talents."

Soyer looked surprised. "You are not speaking to an ordinary man, Miss Nightingale. There are some who can merely cook. But I can make rabbit meat taste like venison. And I could share my secrets with others, too."

"Oh, if that were really true!" Florence sighed and again sipped from her cup. "These patients remaining want so to join their comrades returning home. With good nourishment, they could do so more rapidly. If you could instruct a team of chefs, we could send the chefs to other hospitals."

"When shall we begin, my dear lady? Would tomorrow be soon enough?"

In prayer that evening, Florence felt a twinge of guilt. "Please forgive me, Lord, for feeding Mister Soyer's vanity. But I do so wish to see the men return home soon. I have no doubt that you have sent Mister Soyer for that purpose."

Florence's plan worked. Within days Alexis Soyer was sending trained cooks to hospitals everywhere along the Crimean battle fronts. His students taught others. More rapidly than ever, the soldiers headed home.

The nurses, too, were bidding farewell to the battle fronts. With each one, Florence sent a loving goodbye.

"What you have done for the work," she wrote to Reverend Mother of the Bermondsey nuns, "no one can ever say. My love and gratitude will be yours, dearest Reverend Mother, wherever you go."

Another helper, Miss Shaw-Stewart, had taken charge of nursing at the Castle Hospital. Her zealous spirit had led many to think she was mentally deranged. Yet Florence wrote, "Without her, our Crimean world would have come to grief—without her judgment, her devotion, her unselfish, consistent looking to the one great end . . . her accuracy in all trusts and accounts, her truth, her faithfulness.

Florence tried to visit personally with each nurse before she sailed for England. To many, especially those returning to gloomy, poor lives, Florence gave envelopes containing money from her personal funds. One nurse, a former farm worker, had raised a buffalo calf behind the Barrack Hospital.

"And you'll be taking your friend with you, Miss Evans," Florence told the surprised nurse. "We've managed to secure free passage for the calf."

"You truly are a queen!" Jane Evans exclaimed. "Just like all the soldiers say."

But Florence wanted no thanks or praise. She requested that each nurse not talk to the newspapers about their work, claiming that "we did not come for glory and fame." The nurses agreed.

On July 16, 1856, the last patient left the Barrack Hospital. But Florence's thoughts were not on those soldiers who had gone home. Instead, she wrote "I am a bad mother to come home and leave you in your Crimean graves—seventy-three percent in eight regiments in six months from diseases alone—who thinks of that now?"

As Florence Nightingale packed her bags, *she* thought of that. And she promised that when she got home, she would indeed do something about it.

Homecoming

"Have you heard the news? Miss Nightingale is coming home!"

"Yes, the *London Times* says she's going to sail the last week in July."

"I hear the queen is going to send a battleship to bring her back."

"But she's refused it. She said that everyone should be grateful to the soldiers and not to her. Isn't that just like her? Never seems to want any reward."

Throughout England, people gathered to talk of the return of their wonderful Miss Nightingale. Committees were formed to plan parties. Bands rehearsed so they might meet her. Organizations selected the awards they might give her.

But Florence told no one her plans. She decided to call herself "Miss Smith" and wear a disguise of heavy dark veils. Her plan worked.

Florence landed in England unnoticed and traveled to Lea Hurst. She sighed her relief at finding the depot deserted. She reached home before the family housekeeper came running out the front door.

"Miss Florence! Miss Florence!"

The two old friends embraced and hurried into the house. For hours the Nightingales chattered until Florence was forced to excuse herself. The trip had been long. It was time for a rest.

There was little time for rest during the next few weeks. Relatives, friends, and neighbors streamed into the Nightingale home at Lea Hurst. Presents arrived from all over England. Everyone wanted to show his love for England's wonderful heroine.

"The inns in the village are overflowing," Parthe announced after a day's shopping. "And speaking of overflowing, what are you going to do with all of these gifts?"

Florence glanced around at the living room. It was packed with statues, small items of furniture, beautiful cutlery. Closet space was all filled. Even the bedrooms boasted new decorations.

Mr. Nightingale entered the room and sank down into his favorite chair. Slowly he hoisted his foot onto the footstool.

"Father, what happened?" Parthe asked, watching her father unroll the massive bandage he had wrapped around his big toe.

"Don't worry. The injury is not serious. As I entered the house last evening, I momentarily forgot the lovely new doorstop we display on our porch. Not until I found myself sprawled on my face did I remember."

Parthe and Florence had to force themselves to keep from laughing. Ever since Mr. Bailey, one of the Nightingale neighbors, had presented Florence with the horrid piece of marble to hold the door open, Mr. Nightingale had threatened to leave the house forever. The doorstop was a strange-looking piece of sculpture, which combined features of a horse, a swan, and a butterfly. The result was a three-foot-high monstrosity.

"But surely you would not suggest we return the gift," Florence teased.

"If we did, I am afraid Mr. Bailey would think I was angry at having him beat me at cribbage each Saturday," Mr. Nightingale replied. "No, we must find some other way. Should another war ever occur, I am certain we could give it to the War Office. Surely the enemy would flee if they were to see that atrocious object!"

Parthe, Florence, and their father laughed openly at the idea. Strangely enough, the next morning the marble doorstop was found sitting in the parlor closet. Only on Saturday afternoons, when Mr. Bailey came for the weekly cribbage game, did it sit in the doorway.

Though it was wonderful to be among her family and friends, Florence could not find complete rest. The sights and scenes of battle frequently passed through her mind. At night, she paced the floors recalling the terrible times at Scutari. Often she flicked through the pages of her diary, where she had kept a record of her war activities. Always she would pause at the entry she wrote so many years before.

"February 7, 1837—God spoke to me and called me to His service." Suddenly she realized what was wrong. Her service in the Crimea was just the beginning. There was more to do.

"But you have done your part," Parthe urged. "You must rest. Enjoy the affection the people feel toward you."

"I cannot rest," Florence answered. "The changes that were made in the hospitals at the Crimea should be made all over England. I should be working now while the people still might listen to me. If I wait, people will forget the awful stories of the Crimean War front. I can't forget the men who died because we wouldn't spend money or because people were careless. I stand at the altar of murdered men. While I live, I fight their cause."

With new determination, Florence wrote to the English War Office. She suggested changes—many changes. But Sidney Herbert was no longer War Secretary. In his place sat a new man with different ideas. He hated changes and refused to grant Florence an interview.

"The nerve of that man!" Parthe exclaimed as Florence related the results of her letter. "You spend years helping them at the battlefront and then he won't even listen to you."

"There are other ways," Florence said. "I shall find another way of making my suggestions."

The reluctance of the War Office to listen to Florence saddened her. She knew that if there were to be changes made in the care and treatment of hospital patients, the British War Office would have to lead the way. There seemed to be no hope left.

But a surprise invitation changed everything.

"Queen Victoria has invited me to visit her at Balmoral Castle in Scotland," Florence told her family. "She wants to hear about the work and hospitals at Scutari."

Quickly Florence packed her bags and traveled north to Scotland. The beautiful yet rugged hillsides of the Scottish soil made Florence feel refreshed. As her carriage rolled up the pathway to Balmoral Castle, Florence could feel her heart dancing. She clutched at the sparkling pin she wore on her dress. Queen Victoria had sent it to her while Florence was at the battlefront. It was a lovely piece of jewelry containing dazzling diamonds and shining gold. The inscription, "Blessed are the merciful," meant much to

Florence. Holding the pin seemed to give her renewed strength.

Once in Balmoral, Florence completely relaxed. Queen Victoria and her husband, Prince Albert, were friendly and charming. Hours slipped by as the three talked about the tragedies of the Crimean War. The queen and her husband were shocked by the true stories of the war. They promised they would do all they could to improve hospital conditions in England.

"We really appreciate all you have told us, Miss Nightingale," Prince Albert said quietly. "It is terrible to think how so many must have suffered while defending their country."

"It's fantastic how much you can remember," the Queen exclaimed. "Should you ever need a position, I am certain the War Office would be grateful for your services."

"Not at the present time, I'm afraid. Lord Panure, the new War Office Secretary, and I have exchanged words, not too pleasant ones, I'm afraid."

"Let us ask him to come here," Prince Albert suggested. "Perhaps with these surroundings, we can all be in a more friendly spirit."

Within a few days, Lord Panure joined the group. He was surprised when he met Florence. He had thought she was some loud and bossy woman seeking publicity. When Lord Panure found Florence wanted nothing for herself, he immediately began listening and helping.

"I think a group of men should be formed to investigate everything about the health of the English soldier—during both war and peace," Florence suggested.

"A wise idea," Lord Panure answered. "Perhaps Dr. John Hall might be chairman."

The name of Dr. Hall sent an icy chill through
Florence. How well she remembered his stubborn
actions at the Crimean battlefront.

"I was going to suggest Sidney Herbert," Florence
offered. "He is well acquainted with the present
situation."

Now it was Lord Panure who felt the icy chill. He
had no friendship with Sidney Herbert. Sir Sidney
was too well liked, and Lord Panure was suspicious
of popular men in the government. He was too afraid
of losing his position.

"Let us let the queen decide," Florence compro-
mised. "She knows both men well."

"Agreed."

Queen Victoria made her choice quickly. There was
no doubt as to who would do the job best.

"Sir Sidney Herbert shall be the chairman," Queen
Victoria announced. "And I think Miss Nightingale
is best suited for choosing the other men to serve."

After a month at Balmoral, Florence went home.
She knew another battle lay before her—perhaps more
tiring than the Crimean War itself.

By May of 1857, the Royal Commission (the group
organized to investigate military hospitals), was ready
to hold its first meetings. Often Lord Panure had
slowed the pace to get started, but Florence kept prod-
ding until he was forced to call the meeting.

Witnesses streamed in to testify before the Royal
Commission. Former soldiers, doctors, politicians—all
were called to present their ideas and opinions. But
Florence didn't testify. It wasn't considered ladylike,
and so she sent her written report. It was read aloud
to those present.

"We're fortunate that we had Miss Nightingale's
report," one of the investigators said. "We'd never
have known the complete truth behind the Crimean

hospital situation. Now we can start making changes.''

As the Royal Commission listened to stories of the past, Florence Nightingale made plans for the future. Much of her work was done from a couch, as her attack of Crimean Fever had left her weak and worn. Yet she busily gathered her notes and sent them off to be published.

When the Royal Commission had finished its investigation, a full report was sent to Lord Panure. Florence was pleased with the many suggestions offered by the investigators. She anxiously awaited the changes she hoped would occur.

But the changes did not come.

''I can't understand it, Sidney. You men worked so very hard. Why doesn't Lord Panure take your suggestions?'' Florence stood before her tired friend in his office.

''Florence, I think you will find that sometimes men

are slow to accept suggestions they wished they had
made themselves.''

"But how foolish!''

"But true, nonetheless,'' Sir Sidney consoled.

"We can't give up, Sidney. We must fight this war
like any other. Surely, in time, Lord Panure will
realize we are right.''

Lord Panure would not budge from his stubborn
position. Florence began to lose hope when. . . .

"Florence, did you hear?'' Parthe ran to her sister's
bedside at Lea Hurst. "The House of Commons has
failed to give the government a vote of confidence.
That means all the officials will be out, even Lord
Panure.''

"Oh, Parthe. I did so hope Lord Panure would
come around to our way of thinking. But if he would
not, perhaps this is the way it was meant to be!''

For several days there was much speculation as to
who should be the new Secretary of War. Finally, the
news came.

"Parthe! Mother!'' Florence called. "Sidney
Herbert has been appointed the new War Secretary!''

"Oh, Florence, what could be better!''

Immediately Sidney Herbert began making
changes. Standards of heating, lighting, and ventila-
tion were established for all army hospitals. Special
attention was given the foods and diets for sick
patients. A medical school was started for future
medical officers. From her couch, Florence sent letter after letter to Sidney Herbert. He took action on
almost every suggestion she made.

Florence published a book titled *Notes on Hospitals*.
Shortly afterward, she wrote and published *Notes on
Nursing*. Both books immediately sold thousands of
copies. The money she received went into the
Nightingale Fund, while the books she wrote found

their places in hospitals and homes all over England.

Florence's health was almost gone. Parthe and her mother begged her to rest. Still Florence continued working.

"But you are tired. You must rest," Parthe pleaded.

"Not yet," Florence replied. "There is work left to finish."

Dilemmas and Doubts

"Flo! Oh, Flo!"

Florence glanced up from her writing desk. "What is it, Parthe? Is something wrong?"

"No, no. But a lovely letter has just arrived from the Wilson family in America."

"I hardly think that is cause for your outburst. I thought for a moment the entire house was collapsing."

"Oh, Florence. Let me read this from the letter Clara Wilson has mailed to us. The American poet Henry Wadsworth Longfellow has written about you working with the men at the warfront. Listen to this!

"Lo! in that hour of misery
A lady with a lamp I see
   Pass through the glimmering gloom,
   And flit from room to room.
And slow, as in a dream of bliss,
The speechless sufferer turns to kiss
Her shadow, as it falls
Upon the darkening walls."

Parthe stopped, studying her sister for a reaction. Florence simply raised her quill pen and continued writing.

"Isn't it lovely?" asked Parthe.

"It is silliness and nonsense!" Florence answered.

Stunned, Parthe gazed down at the paper she held tightly in her hand. Carefully, she reread the words to herself. "Oh, Flo, you have to be touched by this man's feelings."

Once more Florence set her pen aside. She looked at her sister with a set jaw and fiery eyes.

"Parthe, that a man raises a pen and creates some wistful image of a saintly creation is of little meaning to me. Now if that man be a government official and he chooses to improve the conditions of a soldier or nurse, that has meaning."

Parthe shook her head in disbelief.

"Surely you were touched by the lovely song, 'The Nightingale of the East.' Oh, dear Flo, I carry a copy of the verse with me everywhere and sing it often."

Without encouragement, Parthe swirled her skirts to the piano bench and seated herself. Flo lifted the piece of paper she had been writing upon and tried to ignore her sister. Softly Parthe began to play the notes of "Cottage and the Wind Mill." Clearing her throat, she began to sing:

Her heart it means good for no bounty she'll take,
She'd lay down her life for the poor soldier's sake;
She prays for the dying, she gives peace to the
   brave,
She feels that the soldier has a soul to be saved,
The wounded they love her as it has been seen.
She's the soldier's preserver, they call her their
   Queen.
May God give her strength, and her heart never fail
One of Heaven's best gifts is Miss Nightingale.

Florence could not listen to another word. Angrily she slammed the paper on the top of the writing desk. "Parthe, one more word of such foolishness and I will set that piano ablaze. Tear that ridiculous poem into one thousand pieces and let the words vanish from that empty head of yours."

Parthe rose from the piano bench with mock indignation. "Well! I just might do some writing of my own this afternoon. I think I shall pen a letter to Mr. Longfellow in America and tell him he need not write any more lines about that ungrateful Florence Nightingale."

Florence nodded. "Please do. And when you have finished, please sign my name to it."

The anger Florence felt about such tributes was not artificial. She could see little use to such efforts. Fortunately she was spared viewing many of the products that found their way to shelves and tables across England.

A figurine from Staffordshire depicted her dressed in a long, flowing white flowered skirt, a blue bodice and a pick bow, and wearing red slippers. Instead of carrying her usual night lamp, she balanced a small tray, two dainty cups resting on it.

Canvas portraits conveyed little likeness of Florence as they found their way to home display and wall hangings. In one, she appeared as a dark native girl wearing a delicate Spanish comb in dark hair. Another print captured her as golden haired, surrounded by roses.

Citizens were not content with porcelain statues and paintings. Sometimes her likeness appeared on giant murals upon the walls of taverns. Her face was carved into ivory cameo brooches and pins. Songs told of her love and kindness; poems recounted her courage and daring.

Florence would have none of it.

"You request permission to write a song of my work at the battlefront hospitals at Scutari," she wrote to one gentleman. "I would suggest your time and talents be better spent writing of the true bravery and valour at that location. Tell of men with torn bodies and spirit who fought nobly for their country, in battle and sick bed. Tell of men faithfully sending their pay orders home to family and loved ones. Tell of men who would leave off drinking for lectures, books, games, and amusements. Tell of men who would work and suffer in silence. This should be your song, dear friend. I was but a witness to greatness and courage. People should sing of participants, not of witnesses."

Florence soon found how quickly a war could be forgotten. People did not want to look back on the ugliness of death and hardship. Instead, they merely wanted to glamorize the fighting and battles. Desperately Florence sought to cast a spotlight on the tragic cost of the Crimean disaster. Letters poured from her writing desk.

"When will our authorities realize that the deaths of thousands of our men were caused by our own inaction?" she wrote to Sidney Herbert. "If only each of the officials who have the power to make corrections could have held the hand of a dying boy, or seen the bloodsoaked uniforms, or inhaled night after night the smell of death!"

But Florence faced two obstacles which she could not change.

First of all, she was a woman. Secondly, she was a national heroine. Powerful men of medicine were jealous of the attention she received. Had many of them not journeyed to the Crimea? Had they not worked long hours and endless nights? Where was their recognition and glory?

"Let them have the fame and attention," Florence declared. "May a throne be given to each man in the British War Office who would help make life better for our soldiers. I pray to God our Father and the Lord our Savior that war shall never come to us again. But should such calamity befall us, let us be prepared."

With each change in the British War Office, Florence had two more suggestions. Nothing moved rapidly enough. Often Florence wished she were a man so people would be more attentive.

Her letters sent to Lord Panure, the Secretary of State for War, brought little response. "Surely you should concern yourself with regaining your own strength," he wrote. "You have brought so many renewed health. Look now to your own well-being."

Even her good friend, Sidney Herbert, encouraged her to rest. "Follow the advice of the doctors—don't read, don't write, don't even think."

One morning, shortly after Florence had arisen, the housekeeper brought in the mail. Mrs. Watson shook her head at Florence.

"How tired you look, child!" the old housekeeper declared. "I would better serve you by pitching this entire post into a burning fire."

"If there is burning to be done, simply burn those foolish notions. Please, let me see what has arrived."

Florence flipped through the letters eagerly. Always her attention turned first to official envelopes bearing the inscriptions of government agencies and officials. But this morning, a fine bonded envelope displaying elaborate script caught her eye. Quickly she tore open the container.

My dearest Miss Nightingale,

Surely you must tire of seeking the glow of public and private attention, as indeed the people of this great empire grow tired of you. Will your voice never

be silent? Have you not enjoyed enough attention
that you must constantly seek more? If the deeds be
true of your service at the Crimea, your efforts were
directed by God. But only the Devil controls such
a wagging tongue as you now have grown.

The letter was unsigned. Florence let the piece of
paper slip from her fingers to the floor. Tears filled
her eyes.

"Are you all right, Miss Florence?" Mrs. Watson
nervously rubbed her hands into her apron.

Florence nodded. "Please, just leave me alone."

Reluctantly, Mrs. Watson left the room. She
glanced back from the doorway, then hurried away
to find Parthe.

Is this what people think? Florence wondered. Do
they truthfully believe my efforts are for myself?

Moments later, Parthe came in. Florence refused
to show her sister the letter which had troubled her
so much.

"Then please return to bed," Parthe ordered. "I
cannot stand to see you so pale and unhappy. You
have been exhausted ever since you came home. We
just won't have it."

Florence did not put up a battle. In fact, she even
consented to travel to Malvern, a quiet village in
western England where people went for rest cures. She
insisted on traveling alone.

The doctors at Malvern could not find any specific
disease. The Crimean Fever had taken its toll, but
nothing more appeared to be wrong.

"You are of delicate constitution, Miss
Nightingale," one doctor told her. "You must take
better care of yourself. Get more rest and worry less
about problems of which you have no control."

The advice frustrated Florence. Did no one

understand her purpose in life? Or had she misunderstood God's direction? As always, she turned to her Creator for help.

"If You would have my tongue be silent, take me to You," she prayed. "If You would have me carry on as I have done, please give me strength and assistance."

Slowly the strength returned. Florence accepted the change as God's will and returned to London. With new energy, she began making appointments and continued writing letters. The unsigned letter was torn up and forgotten.

Florence accepted new tasks. She expanded her interests to British soldiers serving in India and to the Indian people living under British rule. She increased her correspondence, trying to make certain the War Office did not overlook their military men beyond the country's boundaries.

Weary of her family's constant concern and urging "to rest," Florence took rooms at the Burlington Hotel in London. She wanted to dedicate herself to her work and to avoid interruptions.

"I love each and all of you dearly," she wrote home, "but I must be free to carry out the duties God has given me."

Aunt Mai was still received when she visited, and Mr. Nightingale was always welcomed. However, Parthe and Mrs. Nightingale were politely requested to stay away. Florence wanted none of their hand wringing and "flusterings."

While she concentrated on her work, another visitor called on Florence regularly at the Burlington. A widower of fifty-six, Sir Harry Verney was a member of Parliament, rich and handsome. He had taken a keen interest in many of Florence's suggested reforms, speaking out publicly in their behalf.

"He is the voice I need so badly," Florence confided to Selina Bracebridge. "Such a good man he is. Did you know that on his Buckinghamshire Estate, he had founded schools and built model cottages for the poor? We share so many of the same thoughts."

Selina smiled. "That is not all Sir Harry may be interested in sharing, my dear."

Surprised, Florence could not believe what her friend might be suggesting. "You don't think Sir Harry is interested in—in me personally?"

"Would that thought really startle you so much, Florence? You are an admired woman who displays not only a pleasant appearance but a quick mind as well."

"Hm-m-m. It never occured to me."

It had been a long time since Richard Monckton Milnes had come courting. Could it be that Sir Harry Verney had romance as well as reforms in his thinking?

The answer was not long in coming.

"You would greatly honor me by becoming my wife," the widower announced one evening after dinner. "I hope the request in no way dishonors you."

Staring across the table, Florence shook her head. "Hardly that. It is an honor to be asked by such a fine gentleman."

"Then your answer *is*?"

For a moment Florence hesitated. There was so much goodness in this man, so much kindness and warmth.

"Sir Harry, I must decline. And in declining, may I quickly state that your request is as great a compliment as I could ever hope to receive."

The puzzled look in Sir Harry's eyes reflected his confusion. A further explanation was needed.

"A long time ago, I felt a calling to God's

service," Florence explained, rising from the table and walking to the window. "That calling took me to the Crimea, where I felt I was of use."

"Those days are past, Florence."

"Ah, yes, the days at the Crimea are past. And I hope no others like them ever come again. But the calling is still within me. There is more work to be done."

"Could I not help?"

Florence nodded. "Oh, you have already. I hope you will continue to help in the work that needs to be done. But I need your help as a friend, a loving friend. My work must come first. I must do it alone."

For several minutes they said nothing. Finally, Sir Harry stood up. He extended his hands, taking Florence's within his own.

"I accept your decision, Florence, with disappointment and reluctance."

Florence looked hopefully into Sir Harry's face. "And I hope with understanding?" she murmured.

"Yes." He nodded. "With understanding too."

When Mrs. Nightingale learned of the situation, she was totally bewildered. She began inviting Sir Harry to Embley Park to console him. Within months, the gentle widower found himself in love with another Nightingale—Parthe.

"You may be coming to a wedding soon," Aunt Mai told Florence during one of her visits. "Parthe has already begun calling herself 'Lady Verney.' "

"How does Mother take to the idea?"

"She is overjoyed, I believe."

"It does not trouble her that Sir Harry is so much older than Parthe and has four grown children?"

"Not that I can see."

"Good. I am happy for all of them."

On a June day, Parthe and Sir Harry Verney were

married at Embley Park. "Lord, bless their union with love and joy," Florence whispered to herself as she sat watching.

With her family caught up in the excitement of getting to know its latest addition, Florence was free to pursue her work with fresh energy. To her rooms at the Burlington came an unending flow of officials from the government. Daily meetings were held, ideas exchanged, new proposals drawn up.

Finally, Florence sensed that people were listening. She submitted her thoughts about hospital construction, soldier menu and diets, sanitation techniques, suggestions for improving the entire British War Office. The earlier changes that had gained acceptance became sweeping, complete new programs. No longer would the British soldier be regarded and treated as some kind of lowly creature. He was now regarded as a symbol of pride, a worthy subject of the realm to be treated with respect and honor. She had won the battle with officials and officers that soldiers should be treated as loyal deserving men.

Only one final task remained.

"Nursing, professional nursing, must be lifted to the true position that God wishes it to be," Florence wrote to a friend. "If it takes all of my strength, I shall pay the price to put it there."

A Final Task

"Why do you want a school for nurses?"

Florence had heard the question often. The idea of opening a school for nurses was shocking to many people, especially to doctors.

"Nurses are servants!" one doctor declared in Florence's presence. "You would not spend money to train a servant. Why you would spend money to train a nurse, I can't understand."

"Nurses could become much more than servants if they were trained," Florence protested. "Too many people feel that a female nurse cannot understand medicine."

"Well, can they?" the doctor said with a sly smirk.

"If they were taught. Did you understand medicine before you studied it?"

"But men are different. They can learn—"

"So can women!" Florence interrupted. "They can read books and study in classrooms. We must have a formal program of nursing education and training. How can you say it is hopeless?"

"Miss Nightingale, I can see you are a woman of strong opinion. I somehow feel that you will open a nursing home regardless of what is said against such a plan. I had better cease this argument or you will next suggest that women take up the profession of medicine as doctors."

"One thing at a time," replied Florence. "But that idea is not so ridiculous. There will come a day when we will have women doctors."

Florence's final prediction was *too* shocking. Women doctors? Never!

For several months, Florence looked for a hospital which she could use as part of the first school for nurses. She wanted to have the nurses' school close to a hospital so the nursing students might put their learning into practice. Offers from hospitals poured in, for it was well known that the Nightingale Fund was worth over $200,000.

Florence carefully read each letter from every hospital. She wanted to make no mistake!

"This letter sounds quite interesting," Florence remarked to her family one day. "St. Thomas's in London offers us an entire wing of the building for the nurses. Most of the doctors are favorable to the idea, or at least the letter says so. I wonder. . ."

"Why don't you visit St. Thomas's?" Parthe suggested.

"I think I will," Florence answered. "I have to make certain that the woman in charge of the nurses would be a good choice."

Florence learned her answer soon.

"I'm Mrs. Wardroper, Miss Nightingale. It's an honor to meet you."

Seated behind a desk in her office in St. Thomas's Hospital was a tiny woman dressed in black. As Florence seated herself, she immediately noticed the woman wore a pair of dark kid gloves.

"Thank you, Mrs. Wardroper. I'm pleased to meet you. From what I have seen of your hospital, I can say I am quite impressed."

"I hope you can stay with us for a while, Miss Nightingale. I think you should see the hospital closely before making any decisions."

"I agree, Mrs. Wardroper. I'd like to stay."

For the next six months, Florence remained at St. Thomas's. She watched closely every phase of the hospital's functioning. Florence was impressed with everything—most of all, with Mrs. Wardroper. The small woman scurried everywhere, never seeming to be tired.

"I think St. Thomas's will be fine for the nurses' school," Florence told Mrs. Wardroper. "And I think you'll be wonderful as the Superintendent of Nurses. I only wish I were in better health so that I might study with you."

"Your advice will always be welcome," Mrs. Wardroper answered.

In June of 1860, fifteen nervous young women began their training at the Nightingale School for Nurses. The training period would last one year. To some of the trainees, it would seem like ten years.

The rules were strict. Each girl was carefully observed by Mrs. Wardroper. Every month she sent Florence a detailed report of each trainee's actions. The reports revealed even the slightest flaw in hospital care displayed by the student nurses.

"You are the first nurses ever to receive professional training," Mrs. Wardroper told the fifteen students in a lecture. "Miss Nightingale is paying for your food, your housing, your laundry. You must repay Miss Nightingale by doing your very best at all times."

Arising at 6:00 in the morning, the student nurses

plowed through a rigorous daily schedule until 8:30 at night. Beds were changed, patients bathed, medical progress recorded, patients fed, dishes washed, wards dusted and cleaned, doctors assisted, daily lectures attended—all in twenty-four short hours.

Not only was the daily schedule difficult, there were other rules that had to be followed. Mrs. Wardroper not only demanded the nurses learn all about modern nursing, she also demanded they be ladies!

"There is to be no flirting with any of the male medical students," she scolded one of the students. "Your mind, at all times, must be on your work."

By the end of the first year, thirteen of the original fifteen young women graduated. Modern nursing had been born!

Florence had little time to enjoy the graduation of the first class of Nightingale nurses before sad news arrived. Sidney Herbert, her dear friend and supporter, died August 2, 1861.

"I feel so lonely and lost," Florence wrote to a friend. "Always he was there to aid and assist. I pray our Lord and Savior will fill the void within me."

A plea for help from across the sea pulled Florence from her grief. A Civil War had broken out in America, turning peaceful plains and pastures into bloody battlefields. President Lincoln's Secretary of War asked Florence to help organize hospitals and nursing provisions for the injured soldiers.

From her couch in London, Florence sent letter after letter, carefully explaining how to enlist volunteer nurses, how to train them quickly, ways of setting up emergency food programs and proper cooking techniques. Eagerly the American officials followed each suggestion. There was no question about what women could or could not do. Florence's nurses had proven themselves in the Crimea.

In October of 1865, Florence settled into her own home in Mayfair near the center of London. Her own health so delicate she could seldom go out, Florence welcomed a constant stream of visitors. Physicians, government officials, and other nurses made their way to her friendly quarters.

"We need your help," one member of Parliament asked. "We are trying to improve conditions in workhouses and asylums."

"But I do not know enough about such conditions," Florence objected.

"We shall make you aware of the conditions, Miss Nightingale. But we need a woman of your influence on our side. Please help us."

Again and again Florence helped to make needed changes. New programs helped the poor, the mentally ill, and children. For the first time, women were allowed to own property in their own name.

But it was nursing that dominated Florence's thoughts. In 1871 the new St. Thomas's Hospital was completed. Queen Victoria was there to open the facility, while Florence supervised the opening of the Nightingale Training School for Nurses.

Each student enrolled in the school had a personal interview with Florence. She wanted to make sure each nurse-to-be met the high standards necessary for the nursing profession.

"And if you have any suggestions of how the school can be improved," Florence told each visitor, "please let us know. We hope you will learn from us; we will also learn from you."

Florence took special care to see that each graduate nurse was carefully placed. Requests for Nightingale nurses flowed into the school. Florence studied each request, making certain the student seemed suited for the assignment.

"They are my children," Florence told a friend. "You would not want your children sad and unhappy in some faraway place. Nor do I."

If Florence learned one of her nurses was ill, special foods and flowers were sent. Sometimes she opened her own home to a sick nurse, supervising her care and diet.

Nightingale nurses found themselves scattered in locations all over the world. In every place they went, they accepted leadership roles in hospitals and nursing schools. From Canada, the United States, Germany, India, Australia—from tiny towns and major cities—the letters poured into the small apartment in Mayfair.

Eagerly Florence wrote back. Most of her letters ended with "Should there be anything in which I can be of the least use, here I am." Often she enclosed a lovely lace handkerchief or a small sachet of perfumed powder.

Although Florence was satisfied with the program for training her nurses, she insisted they keep up-to-date. By the early 1880's anesthetics were used to control pain. Antiseptics were used to prevent infection. Advances in disease treatment and cure were being made constantly.

"For us who nurse," Florence told her students, "our nursing is a thing in which, unless we are making *progress* every year, every month, every week—take my word for it, we are going *back*. The more experience we gain, the more progress we can make. The progress you make in your year's training with us is as nothing to what you must make every year *after* your year's training is over. A woman who thinks, 'Now I'm a full nurse, a skilled nurse, I have learned all that there is to be learned' does not know what a nurse is, and she will never know. She has slipped back already."

Each student listened closely to the advice Florence shared. To be a Nightingale nurse was truly an honor. But it was a responsibility as well.

In 1893 an admirer of Florence's wrote a promise that would be taken by every person entering the profession of nursing. Lystra Gretter hoped that every future nurse would lead a life of sacrifice, service, and sharing. The promise is called the Florence Nightingale Pledge:

"I solemnly pledge myself before God, and in the presence of this assembly, to pass my life in purity and to practice my profession faithfully. I will abstain from whatever is deleterious and mischievous, and will not take or knowingly administer any harmful drug. I will do all in my power to maintain and elevate the standard of my profession, and will hold in confidence all personal matters committed to my keeping and all family affairs coming to my knowledge in the practice of my calling. With loyalty will I aid the physician in his work, and as a missioner of health, I will dedicate myself to devoted service to human welfare."

Florence smiled as she read the document. Yes, it was a promise worth remembering. She was honored and proud that the pledge would carry her name.

As the years drifted by, the nursing school Florence Nightingale had established became famous all over the world. People came from every country to study the methods used for teaching nurses. Doctors who had laughed at the idea of a nursing school now begged for Nightingale nurses to work with them.

"They're marvelous," one doctor proclaimed. "Sometimes I think these Nightingale nurses could handle the patients by themselves. I only wish we had had Nightingale nurses earlier."

Leaders from many countries heaped praise on Florence. Henri Dunant, the founder of the International Red Cross, credited her with much of his own success.

"Though people praise me for my efforts in establishing the Red Cross," he told a London audience, "it is to one of your own people that all honor is due. The inspiration for my work was Miss Florence Nightingale in the Crimea. Surely she was God's Maiden of Mercy."

Clara Barton, responsible for bringing the Red Cross to America, also praised Florence. "Florence Nightingale was and still is an example for all of us. Never has a person been so totally unselfish in behalf of others. The stories of Miss Nightingale on the Crimean battlefields provided all of us who served as nurses during the Civil War with a shining example of dedication and devotion."

In 1897, the diamond jubilee of Queen Victoria was held. For sixty years, she had reigned over the British

Empire. A great exhibition was held, saluting the progress of nursing during the Victoria reign.

"We would be honored to share any personal belongings of yours within the exhibition," officials wrote to Florence.

Confined to her apartment due to ill health, Florence reluctantly agreed. Writing to a friend, she confessed that she hated "to go on public display." Yet she respected the interest of those who made the request. The exhibition featured a portrait, a head-and-shoulders bust of Florence, and an old lamp.

"The Crimean War was a tragic note in the history of our wonderful country," wrote Florence. "But we learned a great deal from all of our mistakes. The mistakes we made in nursing at the beginning became our foundation for the nursing lessons and programs of the present."

A Special Guest

"Silly notions! Never seen the like of it! Tidy this and tidy that!"

"Miss Whitlow, am I supposed to hear those mumblings of yours?" Florence lifted herself on her sitting couch, straightening the piles of letters she had arranged neatly on her lap. "You have been flitting around here all morning. Obviously, you do not approve of the guest who is coming to tea. You certainly have made that point very clear."

"Hmmph-ph!" came the annoyed answer.

"Hmmph, indeed!" Florence chuckled. "Now that you have watered the flowers on the balcony twice, Miss Whitlow, you might water those in the stand beside the window. I believe they are so thirsty they soon may be grabbing the watering can right from your very hands."

The small, chubby housenurse proceeded to the task given her. But the stiffness in Miss Whitlow's manner did not relax. Slowly Florence lifted herself from the couch, carefully putting the letters on a tray nearby.

"I'm sorry, Miss Nightingale, but I just don't understand you at all. A good Christian woman like yourself . . ."

Miss Whitlow's outburst took Florence by surprise. A good judge of character, she could not imagine what the housenurse was suggesting.

"You think I am unchristian in having the Aga Khan to tea?" Florence asked.

"Well, I don't suppose it's for me to say, but since you ask me, I do find it a bit strange."

"Miss Whitlow, in truth, I feel I owe you no explanation for anything I choose to do. But perhaps because you are so young, you have some mistaken ideas in your mind. Now I am grateful that your superiors at St. Thomas's have loaned you out for my assistance today. Yet I am wondering if that assistance will be useful. It will clearly not be so if you choose to mumble and complain while the Aga Khan is seated with me in the drawing room."

"Well," Miss Whitlow inhaled, her flushed cheeks matching the red curls which stuck outside her lace cap. "It's just that a few of us were talking last night. One of the girls said she understood the Moslem faith to be one which worships demons. Another girl said these people worship in masks."

"Oh, for goodness sake!" Florence exclaimed. "Perhaps if a few of you girls would spend more time reading and less time chattering like chimney wrens, you would not be spreading so much nonsense."

"But—"

Florence raised her hand. "No, Miss Whitlow. You have shared ignorance enough, and I wish to hear no more. The Aga Khan is the leader of the Moslem or Islam faith. Moslems don't believe in Jesus, it's true. They think Mohammed is the prophet God chose to lead their religion. The Moslems believe they should submit themselves to God, and that heaven and hell await them after a final judgment.

"But what about having to worship in masks?"

"Not masks, my dear, but mosques. A mosque is what they call the buildings they worship in."

Miss Whitlow sat silently for several seconds. "I—I see what you mean. Not masks. Not demons. But they do believe differently, don't they?"

Florence smiled. "Yes, they do. But we don't have to be afraid of the Aga Khan. What do you suppose Jesus would do in this situation? I am sure we have all we can do to live our Christian faith in the best manner we can. I know the Aga Khan represents some different beliefs. But whatever the case, I'm sure we will be able to share a cup of tea together."

"I'm sorry, Miss Nightingale."

"Go tend to the tea and desserts, Miss Whitlow. I must tend to my own appearance."

"Tending to appearance" was not an enjoyable chore for Florence in her later years. Her slender frame, tall and graceful in youth, grew stout and pouchy. In younger days, her head had appeared small on a narrow pivoting neck. Now the neck had almost disappeared, and the face had widened.

Carefully Florence ran a comb through the thin strands of hair, parting it as always in the middle. She enjoyed wearing high white collars, often set off by family brooches.

Florence ate a small lunch of soup, then returned to her letter writing while awaiting her guest. She even had time for a light nap. By the time Miss Whitlow appeared to announce the Aga Khan's arrival, Florence was well rested and eager to visit.

As usual, the guest was entertained in the downstairs drawing room. The Aga Khan rose as Florence entered the room.

"You are kind to receive me," the religious leader said. "I feel so very honored to be in your home."

Florence nodded, then sat down. She noted the keen eyes of the man seated across from her. He was alert, noting every movement and listening to every word. The meeting promised to be interesting.

How swiftly the hours slipped by. The Aga Khan proved to be a true student of history. Questions tumbled from his lips like rain from a broken spout.

India was a main topic. Being under British government rule and filled with Moslems, India was dear to both Florence and the Aga Khan. For years Florence had helped direct efforts for better sanitation and nursing programs in the faraway land.

"You have done so much for my people," the Aga Khan said. "You are a special person to them, like a legend."

"A legend," Florence mused. "That makes me feel even older than I am."

"It is a beautiful legend, Miss Nightingale. Beautiful in every way."

"More tea?"

Miss Whitlow stood smiling as she poured the hot liquid into the two porcelain cups. Florence returned the younger woman's smile. It was clear the housenurse's attitude about the guest had changed.

"I hope my visit caused no inconvenience," the Aga Khan offered.

"I would say excitement rather than inconvenience, wouldn't you agree, Miss Whitlow?" Florence asked.

Nodding, Miss Whitlow gave a quick curtsy and left the room.

But not all of the Nightingale nurses proved as easy to impress as Miss Whitlow. Many wished to be registered officially after they had received their training. This would eliminate the untrained and incompetent.

"We need your help," one student nurse told Florence one morning in her apartment. "Nursing is a profession. Would you help us? Until we are considered professional workers, we will never be able to earn the wages we deserve."

Florence raised an eyebrow. Her face reddened.

"Is this why you wish to be a nurse, for the wages?"

Flustered but undaunted, the student nurse looked the older woman directly in the eyes.

"At the present time, Miss Nightingale, there are still many untrained and incompetent individuals who call themselves 'nurses.' We would like to see a Register of Nursing established. To be registered, an individual would need definite training in a school or hospital. We would be protecting the public."

"You did not answer my question, my dear."

"No, I did not enter the profession of nursing for the money." The student nurse gazed down. "I want to help people, like you did. But I *do* believe a person can seek proper pay for professional services. I feel no shame in that."

The girl has spunk, Florence decided. Too idealistic perhaps, a bit confused, but full of spunk.

"I'm afraid, Miss—Miss—I'm sorry, you'll have to forgive an old woman. I've forgotten your name."

"Andrews, Miss Nightingale. Clare Andrews."

"Miss Andrews, you speak with some degree of eloquence. But I'm afraid I shall never accept the idea of nursing only as a profession."

"I beg your pardon?"

Slowly Florence shifted her weight on the couch. She pulled her coverlet higher about her waist.

"I agree that the public should be protected against the untrained and uneducated. Heaven knows, I saw enough of them in my time. But I also believe that nursing is a calling. It is essential that a nurse be of the best spiritual and moral character. What Register of Nursing could determine such qualities?''

"Yes, I agree that—"

"Please, let me finish. I've said that I believe nursing is a calling. I am convinced that to become a nurse, one must be answering a direct call from God. I also believe nursing is an art. Just as a painter devotes himself to creation on canvas or a sculptor carves into cold marble, a nurse dedicates herself to an even greater purpose, for she is working with the living body—the temple of God's spirit.''

Clare Andrews rose from her chair. She slowly made her way to the door. "I had better go, Miss Nightingale.''

"You do understand my feeling?"

"Yes, I believe I do. But I also believe our world is changing. We must change with it.''

"I am no stranger to change, Miss Andrews.''

"Oh, I know, Miss Nightingale. You probably wonder why I was sent here to represent the other student nurses. It is because they compare me to you. If you want something done, have Clare Andrews do it. She's as fiery as the old woman—oh, I'm sorry, Miss Nightingale. I meant no disrespect.''

Florence nodded and smiled. "None taken, Miss Andrews.''

"It's just that I'd hoped to win you over. I wanted you to understand that as nurses, we deserve certain rights.''

Florence shook her head. "That is where we cannot agree, I'm afraid. This 'old woman' never thinks of the rights of nurses. I can only think of their duties, first to God and then to their patients.''

Clare stepped forward. "But aren't rights an insistence upon other people's duties?'' she argued.

Florence waved her hand away. "You are too quick

with your words, Miss Andrews. I cannot keep up with you.''

''I'm sorry,'' the younger woman replied, stepping back. ''I hope I have not discomforted you.''

Florence smiled. ''Child, you have indeed discomforted me. But never feel ashamed of causing discomfort over matters which you feel deeply. I am sorry we cannot agree and I cannot lend you my support.''

''I am, too.''

''But somehow, I sense you may triumph anyway. I have stood where you are now standing, challenging authority. It can be a lonely fight, Miss Andrews, but fight it anyway if it is what you truly believe. If it be God's will, you shall win.''

''Thank you, Miss Nightingale. You have given me strength.''

Each year brought fewer visitors to her apartment. It was Florence's own decision. Cousins, friends, government officials, royalty—all begged to call on the famous ''lady of the lamp.'' But Florence resisted.

''I am now and always have been a far better writer of letters than I am a speaker of words,'' she wrote to one friend. ''There is also the truth that when I tire of writing, I can stop. At times, a lingering guest forces me to yawn. My mother would hardly have approved of such conduct.''

But in time, even the letters slowed. Florence's sight began to fail as the twentieth century dawned. Relatives and friends insisted she accept a live-in companion. She accepted reluctantly. She soon came to enjoy being read to, whether it be daily newspapers, personal letters, or books. When her health began to steadily fail, a full-time nurse was hired. Sometimes it was difficult knowing who was the patient and who was the nurse.

''Miss Nightingale!'' one nurse exclaimed one

morning. "Last night I remember perfectly that I read to you, tucked you in, and blew out the candle before going to bed myself. This morning, when I awakened, I found myself firmly tucked in. Now, unless a stranger entered this apartment in the night and made his way to my sleeping quarters, I feel I must hold *you* accountable."

Florence grinned. "Hm-m-m. Do you think we should have the bolt on the door examined?" she asked.

"Oh, Miss Nightingale, you are impossible!" the nurse declared. But she could not prevent the loving smile from crossing her face.

Snowflakes danced through the streets in London in December of 1907. A carriage rolled over the rugged cobblestones and stopped in front of Florence's apartment. One of the king's secretaries stepped out and entered the building. He carried important news. Florence had received the Order of Merit, the highest award a British citizen could win. It was the first time a woman had been presented the award.

"King Edward VII asked that I speak to you personally," the secretary explained. "He sends his very best wishes for your good health."

Florence nodded. At eighty-seven, she was not able to understand everything around her. "Too kind," she murmured, "too kind."

The following year brought still another honor. She was named to receive the Freedom of the City of London. A nurse helped guide Florence's hand as she signed her initials to the Roll of Honour.

News that Florence was still alive surprised many people when stories reached the newspapers of the recognition she received. Cards and letters flooded the apartment.

"I remember you bringing me soup as I lay in a

hospital bed in Scutari,'' wrote one veteran. ''You
sat beside me and prayed. I shall never forget it. I
told you I wanted to die. 'That is not your decision
to make,' you told me. 'Only God shall choose that
time.' That was fifty-four years ago and I'm still
around. And you are, too. Hooray for the both of us!''

''I am delighted to learn of your recent recognition,'' a nurse wrote from Birmingham. ''There is
no way of knowing how many individuals have
entered the profession of nursing because of your
example. My mother is one and I am also. Now my
ten-year-old daughter has expressed such a desire.
Surely you must be proud of the role you have played
in so many lives.''

Florence smiled and nodded as she listened to the
letters. She dictated replies to a secretary. ''We must
answer every one,'' she said firmly. ''Every one.''

Time to Rest

Summer, 1910.

The people in London suffered day after day of intense heat, with breezes being only a memory from a time long before. Death had ended the reign of Queen Victoria after sixty-four years.

In her ninetieth year, Florence Nightingale was small and frail. Her daily world was limited to the boundaries of her bedroom on South Street. Her eyesight was failing, her hearing weakening.

"God has blessed me with the fulfillment of my heart's longings," she wrote to a friend. "I only hope I may see Him soon to thank Him for all the gifts He has given me."

A housekeeper prepared her meals and a trained nurse looked after her. Florence thought such attention was unnecessary.

"I can tend to my own needs," she declared.

Despite such protests, Florence enjoyed the companionship. Guests dropped in, many of them former nurses wishing to share their own experiences. Often a cat or two had to be shooed off a chair before a guest could sit down. Florence's pet family enjoyed many special privileges provided by their loving owner.

One evening, shortly after retiring for bed, Florence heard sounds outside. Slowly rising and pulling on a robe over her nightgown, Florence crossed to the window. She gazed out at a small cluster of young women. Their voices joined in strong harmony:

> Onward, Christian soldiers,
> Marching as to war
> With the cross of Jesus,
> Going on before.

Florence smiled as she stood listening. She gently pulled back the lace curtain and waved to the carolers. As they sang, Florence's memory was filled with thoughts of the past. She remembered the old nuns of Kaiserwerth, Sidney Herbert, Parthe, Mother, Father—oh, there was so much to recall. Father Manning, Richard Milnes (what kind of a life might she have had with him?), Selina Bracebridge, the Crimea . . . Suddenly Florence heard a bright cheerful melody.

> Oh, we're proud to be Nightingale nurses
> Bringing care and comfort to the ill,
> Oh, we're proud to be Nightingale nurses
> Praying that our lives will be fulfilled.

It was a spritely little lyric, obviously written by the student nurses themselves. They marched away, leaving the smiling woman at her window. Slowly she turned.

"Now it is time to rest," she whispered. "Now it is time to rest."

Florence Nightingale died at her residence, 10 South Street, in London, on Saturday, August 13,

1910. She had lived ninety years and three months.

News of Florence's death traveled quickly through England and to other countries across the sea. In truth, many people thought she had been dead for years. It had been so many years since her heroism at the Crimean warfront!

But her courage had not been forgotten.

"She merits the finest funeral we can give her," wrote one newspaper editor. "We have been blessed with two queens in our British Empire—Victoria and Florence."

"Westminster Abbey would be a suitable final resting place for this splendid angel," another editor wrote. "Surely she should lie among those we honor most."

But Florence had different ideas about such matters. Her will revealed a wish that her remains be donated to medical science for examination, then "carried to the nearest burial ground accompanied by not more than two persons without trappings."

A compromise was reached.

"There will be no national funeral or burial in Westminster Abbey," government officials announced. "However well deserved, such attention would run contrary to the wishes of the late Miss Nightingale."

But neither was the body donated to medical science.

"Our beloved Florence Nightingale lived a life devoted to nursing and medicine," observed a family spokesman. "In death, she will lie in peace."

Six British sergeants, dressed in formal military wear, carried the coffin to a grave beside those of Florence's mother and father near Embley Park. The courtyard was filled with bright, cheerful flowers, just as it had been when Florence was a child. Men, women, children—many of them poorly dressed—stood quietly.

In the afternoon sunlight, a powerful hymn blossomed out among those present. The words of "The Son of God Goes Forth to War" added strength and power to the moment. It had been one of Florence's favorite hymns.

Slowly the villagers left the courtyard. One old soldier, wearing a tattered ribbon of the Crimean Campaign, stopped and glanced back.

"God bless her," he mumbled to his wife.

The old woman took her husband's arm and smiled. "He is probably doing that at this very moment," she said softly.

APPENDIX

Events in the Life of
Florence Nightingale

1820 Born May 12 in Florence, Italy

1837 February 7, Florence records in her diary a call to God's service

1839 May 24, Florence is presented to Queen Victoria

1842 May 10, Florence is introduced to Richard Monckton Milnes

1843 Florence decides to work in hospitals

1844 Florence declines wedding proposal of Richard Monckton Milnes

1845 Florence seeks nurse's training at Salisbury Infirmary, parents voice objection

1847 December, Florence visits hospitals in Rome, Italy, and observes Catholic sisters fulfilling nursing duties

1850 August, Florence visits Kaiserwerth Institution in Germany and observes nursing practices

1851 July, Florence returns to Kaiserwerth and joins in active nursing duties

1853 August 12, Florence becomes Superintendent of the Institution for the Care of Sick Gentlewomen in Distressed Circumstances

1854 March, the Crimean War begins

October, Florence appointed Superintendent of Female Nursing Establishment of English General Hospitals in Turkey

November, Florence and her nurses arrive at Scutari on the Crimean war front

1855   June, Florence contracts Crimean Fever and
        almost dies. Returns to nursing duties after
        recovery

1856   March 30, peace treaty signed, officially
        ending the Crimean War
        August, Florence returns to England
        November, Florence declines wedding pro-
        posal of Sir Harry Verney

1859   Florence publishes *Notes on Hospitals* and
        Notes on Nursing

1860   July 9, Nightingale Training School is opened
        at St. Thomas's Hospital in London

1861   October, Florence assists the United States in
        helping organize soldiers' hospitals during
        the Civil War

1865   Florence settles in her Mayfair home in
        London

1871   June, Florence named head of the Nightingale
        Training School at the new St. Thomas's
        Hospital

1897   Diamond Jubilee of Queen Victoria includes
        exhibition of Florence Nightingale's nursing
        contributions

1907   December, Florence is awarded the Order of
        Merit

1910   August 13, Florence dies in her sleep

The Written Works of Florence Nightingale

The Institution of Kaiserwerth on the Rhine for the
Practical Training of Deaconesses (1851)

Letters from Egypt (1854)

Notes on Matters Affecting the Health, Efficiency and
Hospital Administration of the British Army (1858)

A Contribution to the Sanitary History of the British
Army During the Late War with Russia (1859)

Notes on Hospitals (1859, 1863)

Suggestions for Thought to the Searchers after Truth
among the Artisans of England—Three Volumes
(1860)

Notes on Nursing: What it is, and What it is Not
(1860)

Observations on the Sanitary State of the Army in
India ((1861)

Army Sanitary Administration and its Reform under
the late Lord Herbert (1862)

How People may Live and not Die in India (1856)

On Trained Nursing for the Sick Poor (1876)

Indian Letters, A Glimpse into the Agitation for
Tenancy Reform. Bengal 1878-82 (1937)

Bibliography

Andrews, Mary Shipman. *A Lost Commander: Florence Nightingale*. New York: Doubleday, 1929.

Cook, Sir Edward. *The Life of Florence Nightingale*. New York: The MacMillan Company, 1942.

Cooper, Lettice U. *The Young Florence Nightingale*. New York: Roy Publishers, 1960.

Dodge, Bertha S. *The Story of Nursing*. Boston: Little, Brown and Company, 1954.

Garnett, Emmeline. *Florence Nightingale's Nuns*. New York: Farrar, Straus & Cudahy, 1961.

Nightingale, Florence. *Notes on Nursing: What it is, and What it is not*. (Originally printed in 1859). New York: J.B. Lippincott Company, 1957.

O'Malley, Ida B. *Florence Nightingale 1820-1856*. London: Butterworth & Company, 1931.

Seymer, Lucy Ridgely. *Florence Nightingale*. New York: The MacMillan Company, 1950.

Strachey, Lytton. *Eminent Victorians*. New York: G.P. Putnam's Sons, 1918.

Woodham-Smith, Cecil. *Florence Nightingale*. New York: McGraw-Hill Book Company, 1951.

Woodham-Smith, Cecil. *Lonely Crusader*. New York: Whittlesey House, 1951.

INDEX

SOWERS SERIES

* New title coming soon.